The Weekend

Faced with a family gathering, world-weary Stephen Febble does his best to be difficult. When his daughter, her dreary husband Alan, their precocious child and – not least – the dog come to stay for the weekend it's enough to make him reach for the whisky, and for the sarcasm. The climax arrives on Saturday night when his patient wife Virginia has laid on a dinner party and the chiropodist comes too.

In his first stage play, *The Weekend*, Michael Palin takes a look at family values which is not only very funny but also has its darker side.

The Weekend had its first West End production at the Strand Theatre, London, in spring 1994, starring Richard Wilson.

Michael Palin was born in Sheffield in 1943. He was a founder member of the Monty Python team and has written and performed in numerous successful films and television series, including *The Missionary*, *Time Bandits*, *A Private Function*, *A Fish Called Wanda*, *American Friends* and *GBH*. In addition to the bestselling *Around the World in 80 Days* and *Pole to Pole*, he has written a number of books, notably *Ripping Yarns* with Terry Jones, and several children's books including *The Mirrorstone*, *Small Harry and the Toothache Pills*, *Limericks* and the *Cyril* stories. He lives in North London with his wife and three children.

T0347810

Michael Palin

The Weekend

METHUEN DRAMA

METHUEN DRAMA MODERN PLAYS

First published in Great Britain in 1994
by Methuen Drama

Copyright © 1994 by Michael Palin
The author has asserted his moral rights

ISBN 0 413 68940 9

A CIP catalogue record for this book is available at the British Library.

Typeset by Wilmaset Ltd, Wirral
Transferred to digital printing 2002

The photograph of Richard Wilson as Stephen Febble, on the front cover, is
by Sven Arnstein from the poster for the 1994 production; reproduced by
kind permission of Mr Wilson. The author's photograph on the back is reproduced by kind permission of Basil Pao.

Caution
All rights in this play are strictly reserved and application for performance
etc. should be made to: The Gumby Corporation Ltd, 68a Delancey Street,
London NW1 7RY. No performance may be given unless
a license had been obtained.

This paperback is sold subject to the condition that it shall not, by way of
trade or otherwise, be lent, resold, hired out, or otherwise circulated without
the publisher's prior consent in any form of binding or cover other than that
in which it is published and wthout a similar condition being imposed on the
subsequent purchaser.

The Weekend was first performed at the Yvonne Arnaud Theatre, Guildford, on 15 March 1994 and subsequently at the Strand Theatre, London, on 26 April 1994. It was produced by David Pugh Ltd, Robert Fox Ltd and Archie Stirling Ltd. The cast was as follows:

Stephen Febble	Richard Wilson
Virginia Febble	Angela Thorne
Diana	Julie Peasgood
Alan	Jonathan Coy
Charlotte	Joanna Forest
Duff Gardner	John Ringham
Bridget Gardner	Marcia Warren
Hugh Bedales	Michael Medwin
Mrs Finlay	Yvonne d'Alpra

Directed by Robin Lefevre
Designed by Eileen Diss
Lighting by Leonard Tucker
Costume Supervisor Fizz Jones
Props Supervisor Jane Slattery
Company Manager Trevor Williamson
Deputy Stage Manager Julian Stoneman
Assistant Stage Managers Lee Brooks, Nicola Greenhill, Peter Leafe
Wardrobe Mistress Marie Harper

Characters

Stephen Febble, *retired. Around sixty*
Virginia Febble, *his wife. Younger by eight or nine years*
Diana, *their daughter. In her mid thirties*
Alan, *Diana's husband. A specialist in bulk cargo-handling techniques. Mid thirties*
Charlotte, *their young daughter*
Pippa, *their dog*
Duff Gardner, *a neighbour of the Febbles. Of Stephen's age. Also retired*
Bridget Gardner, *Duff's wife. Mid fifties*
Hugh Bedales, *a society chiropodist*
Mrs Finlay, *a Marxist cleaning lady*
God (*off*)

The action takes place in the **Febbles'** house in Suffolk, in the present day.

Act One

Friday.

The lights come up on a reasonably well-furnished middle-class home on a bright day towards the end of summer. The greater part of the stage is taken up with a drawing room, which has upstage french windows giving on to a garden.

Upstage left is an exit to the front door and hallway. Another door leads to a kitchen. The furniture reflects the comfortable taste of moderately well-off, rather settled occupants in early old age. As it is a fine day the french windows stand open.

A Daily Telegraph *is being read in a large armchair. After a moment the* Daily Telegraph *begins to droop and is suddenly jerked up again. Quite a few moments pass and the paper begins to droop again. This time it goes quite a long way down, revealing the lolling head and closing eyes of* **Stephen Febble**, *as the paper crumples quietly onto his knees.* **Stephen**'s *head falls forward and has just reached comfortable repose when the sound of a telephone ringing in the hallway causes him to jerk into wakefulness rather violently.* **Stephen** *makes no attempt to answer it.*

He retrieves the paper that he's let slip and settles himself authoritatively into a reading position, assiduously ignoring the phone. After a moment footsteps are heard outside. The front door opens and **Stephen**'s *wife,* **Virginia**, *runs into the hall, shouting:*

Virginia I'll get it!

She picks up the phone.

Virginia Canfield 3914 . . . Darling . . . Oh, how *lovely* . . . yes . . . all right darling . . . bye.

Virginia Febble *enters with a shopping bag in one hand. She is about eight years younger than* **Stephen**, *attractive, competent and a touch world-weary.*

Virginia Isn't that wonderful . . . They're coming down at the weekend after all.

Stephen *lowers his paper slowly.*

Stephen *This* weekend?

Virginia Yes . . . tomorrow!

Stephen (*with feeling*) Oh dear God no . . .

Virginia And they're bringing Pippa and Charlotte.

Stephen Oh my God . . . I'm going to emigrate . . .

Virginia To where . . . ?

Stephen Anywhere just anywhere. Possibly the Republic of Dominica.

Virginia There isn't such a place dear.

Stephen There is, or I wouldn't have said it. It's the other half of Haiti . . .

Virginia Isn't that where one of those Evelyn Waugh books was set . . . Haiti?

Stephen No. It used to be Hispaniola. The whole island. Much beloved by pirates and other people who preferred death or scurvy rather than visits from relations.

Virginia *starts to empty her shopping basket.*

Virginia Why do you hate them so much, dear?

Stephen Because they have an incontinent dog for a start.

Virginia Oh, that was ages ago, that was in April.

Stephen The mark is still there.

Virginia Well, what does it matter?

She takes some cut flowers from her shopping bag and carries them into the kitchen.

Stephen It *matters* if I want to go to a college reunion . . . that's *why* it matters!

Virginia (*from the kitchen*) You can wear another tie.

Stephen I can't wear another tie, woman . . . that's the point . . . that tie she crapped on is the Pardoner's Club tie . . . there are only twenty-three in existence . . . that's the point of the club!

Virginia (*off*) What? To preserve old ties . . . ?

Stephen No! To have only twenty-three members . . .

Virginia (*off*) Well, it doesn't show . . .

She appears with cut flowers in a vase and sets them down on a side-table; she stands back and rearranges them.

Stephen It *does* show, it shows on the pale blue bits.

Virginia Use some Dab-it-off . . .

Stephen Dab-it-off leaves marks.

Virginia Of course it doesn't, that's the whole point of Dab-it-off . . .

Stephen How can a dog . . . ?

Virginia Oh, don't start darling, it'll be lunchtime soon . . .

She examines a vaseful of old flowers, and after some thought carries them out to the kitchen as **Stephen** *continues:*

Stephen How can a dog, even taking into account that it's as dim-witted as that one . . . how can a dog with miles of pavements, shopping precincts and children's playgrounds to crap on, choose *my* tie? . . . Mmmm? . . .

Virginia (*off*) There's a bit of cottage pie left and some of Mrs Finlay's tart . . .

Stephen I mean for a dog to hit a tie at all requires some skill you know. That little bastard is a canine Barnes Wallis. The Dambusters would have been proud of him. They'd have put the little bugger in the bomb-bay of a Lancaster, and he could probably have got Hitler right on the side of the head from 16,000 feet. War would have ended in twenty minutes.

Virginia (*reappearing, with the empty vase and setting it down*) You could have it cold with spring onions?

Stephen You're not listening are you . . . ?

Virginia Not really dear . . . or radishes . . . ?

Stephen I don't want spring onions or radishes . . .

Virginia We've got heaps in the garden, they've got to be eaten up . . .

She goes towards the french windows.

Stephen (*after her*) If you ever read anything apart from *Woman's Realm* you would realise that there operates in the world a peculiar economic force known as the law of supply and demand.

She goes out into the garden. He carries on, from his chair.

. . . Were you to have possessed the merest smattering of knowledge about this primary and basic economic tenet you would not have thrown over two bedsful of perfectly good French marigolds and gone over to intensive radish farming! Even if I ate radish salad every hour, *on* the hour, for the next eight weeks, we'd have a radish mountain by the end of this summer that'd make the EEC look understocked.

Virginia (*from the garden*) You're just being difficult because I didn't know where the Dominican Republic was . . .

Stephen It wasn't a question of not knowing where it was, it was a question of not even acknowledging its existence . . .

Virginia *comes in holding a large clump of radishes.*

Virginia Well, I expect I'm not the only one . . .

Stephen No, there'll be your friend Marjorie . . .

Virginia Oh don't let's start about Marjorie.

Virginia *disappears into the kitchen.*

Stephen She's too dim to peel an orange!

There is a pause.

Virginia (*off*) There is some chicken.

Stephen Chicken . . . ooh . . . lovely chicken. I haven't had chicken since . . . let me see now . . . last night.

Virginia (*off*) You're lucky to get lunch, Marjorie sends Rollo down to the pub.

Stephen Oh *dear*! (*He lays on the mock horror.*) What an ordeal . . . the pub for *lunch*!

Virginia (*reappearing*) You know you can go if you want.

Stephen No, it means I have to talk to Rollo . . . I'll have a lager though . . . (*He gets up and walks out to the kitchen.*)

Virginia (*quickly, as she passes him*) It's only eleven.

Stephen (*not breaking his step*) It's eleven . . . eight!

She goes out into the garden.

He walks out to the kitchen where he extracts a can of lager from the fridge. As he is about to re-enter the room, the phone rings in the hall.

Stephen (*tapping on the window*) Telephone!

Virginia *has to hurry in from the garden (with another handful of radishes) to go through to answer it.* **Stephen** *appears, tearing the top off his lager. He puts the lager down beside his armchair and goes across to the drinks cabinet. He is extracting a box of cheese straws when there is a tap on the french window. He looks up, irritated.*

Stephen My God . . . it's like Piccadilly Circus in here . . . Who's that?

A very little lady puts her head deferentially round the door.

Stephen Oh, it's you, Mrs Finlay . . . maker of the famous tarts. Do *you* know where the Dominican Republic is?

Mrs Finlay Oh yes . . . indeed Mr Febble. A friend of my brother's was imprisoned there for six years . . . for reading Gorki on the bus.

Silence.

Stephen What d'you want?

Mrs Finlay I just came to say that my mother's died, so I won't be able to come tomorrow . . .

Stephen Consider yourself lucky Mrs Finlay . . . we've got the mob coming down . . .

Mrs Finlay Miss Diana and Mr Alan . . . ?

Stephen Yes . . . and the cat and the dog and the parrot and the goldfish and the children and the transistor radio and the eighteen gerbils.

Mrs Finlay Oh, that'll be nice for you all . . .

Stephen It'll be horrid. I'm thinking of emigrating this afternoon.

Mrs Finlay Oh, I don't think you can do it as quickly as that Mr Febble. A friend of my brother wanted to emigrate to Libya and it took him eight months to get the papers. He had to have all kinds of injections and . . .

Stephen Libya? Why did he want to emigrate to Libya?

Mrs Finlay Well, of course his first choice was North Yemen, but he failed the medical . . .

Stephen (*suspiciously*) What's wrong with him?

Mrs Finlay Well, that's just it, they don't know . . .

Stephen (*poised to empty the lager into a glass*) Well, what . . . what *sort* of thing?

Mrs Finlay It's in his water. I know that.

Stephen Oh . . . but why did he want to go to Libya?

Mrs Finlay I think he likes the regime there.

Stephen Extraordinary . . . Anyway, I'll tell Mrs Febble you popped in.

Mrs Finlay I'm not just popping in . . . I've come to *do* . . . because I can't come tomorrow . . . because of my mother . . .

Stephen Oh. . .

Mrs Finlay Is it all right . . . ?

Stephen Yes, of course, must have the place clean. Can't have the dog crapping on a dirty carpet . . .

Mrs Finlay Thank you, Mr Febble . . . Sorry to disturb you. I would have come earlier, but there's all the formalities to be gone through, and what with Victor coming over from Ireland –

She's cut short as **Virginia** *comes off the phone and into the sitting room.*

Virginia Hello, Mrs F. . . . how's your mother . . . ?

Stephen *hears this with malicious delight and grunts uncontrollably into his beer.*

Mrs Finlay She's gone.

Virginia Gone?

Mrs Finlay Gone . . . on . . . up . . . over the other side, Mrs Febble . . . Wednesday night.

Virginia Oh, I'm sorry. Still I suppose it was for the best in the end.

Mrs Finlay Oh yes, she wasn't a happy woman. But do you know, Mrs Febble, and I mustn't keep you, because you're all very busy, but right to the end she believed in a Marxist-Leninist solution.

Virginia Well . . .

Mrs Finlay And she was *ninety-three*.

Virginia Well, I am sorry . . . I'm sure you'll miss her.

Mrs Finlay Yes . . . yes . . . I suppose I shall. She was one of a kind. She'd met all the Fabians. She ironed for Rebecca West.

Stephen *shouts impatiently.*

Stephen Virginia!

Mrs Finlay Well I'd best get on.

Stephen (*extravagantly loudly*) Virginia!

Virginia (*coming over to him*) What is it dear?

Stephen Look at the state of this glass!

Virginia *crosses to the sofa where* **Stephen** *holds up the glass and pretends to indicate something.*

Stephen (*confidentially*) Just saving you from that garrulous old ratbag . . .

Virginia Oh come on dear, she's not that bad. We have long chats when you're not here.

Stephen About her brother-in-law's earache . . .

Virginia No, about all sorts of things. Her family's communist, you know . . .

Stephen Damn good thing too . . . only party with any guts.

Virginia There aren't many left now, are there?

Stephen Oh you bet. They've just changed their name to Conservatives. They'll be back.

Virginia Oh well, I suppose there's something to be said for them.

Stephen Oh absolutely. Any party that sends people to the salt mines can't be all bad. These cheese straws are foul.

Virginia They're Marks and Spencer's.

Stephen Oh that's all right then. So long as they're Marks and Spencer's they can taste like an Afghan's armpit . . .

Virginia All I'm saying dear is that they are exactly the same cheese straws that I bought you last week because you were complaining about the ones I got in the village . . .

Stephen Watch out, Stalin's behind you.

Mrs Finlay *stands at the kitchen doorway. She has a headscarf on and a brush in her hand.*

Mrs Finlay Er . . . Mrs Febble . . . shall I do upstairs first . . . as you're in the middle of –

Virginia Oh yes. Could you? Just run over the bedrooms. Only we have Alan and Diana and . . .

Stephen . . . Charlotte and Emma and Pippa and four cats and six gerbils . . .

Virginia . . . coming down for the weekend . . .

Stephen . . . coming for the weekend . . .

Mrs Finlay Oh, that'll be nice for you . . .

Virginia (*to* **Mrs Finlay**) You couldn't help me move the put-you-up into the back bedroom.

A dog barks outside. **Virginia** *and* **Mrs Finlay** *exit.*

After a moment's pause the dog starts to bark nearer and louder. It's shushed heavily. A head appears around the french windows. This is **Duff**. *Another middle-aged man. He wears spectacles and a Panama. His face has an English tan (i.e. it ends at the top of his vest) and he has a light shirt on. It's obviously warm outside. The head looks around for a moment, then the entire body enters. He has long khaki shorts on. There is a loud barking from outside the window.* **Duff** *rushes back.* **Stephen** *jerks round and a look of disgust focuses his features.*

Duff (*off*) BE QUIET! you silly animal . . . we're going home in a minute.

Duff *re-enters.*

Stephen Why don't you have it put down, Duff. It only costs thirty quid. One of the best bargains you can get these days.

Duff Sorry old boy . . . didn't mean to disturb you . . .

Stephen Oh come in. I was only reading the paper. Damned interesting article on sweating.

Duff Oh . . . I must have missed that . . .

Stephen Yes . . . it's very good for you evidently.

Duff Do you sweat a lot, Stephen?

Stephen Me . . . ? Oh I'm pretty average I suppose.

Duff Yes, me too . . . (*Pause.*) . . . Some people aren't though.

Stephen Aren't what?

Duff Aren't average.

Stephen (*positively*) Oh no.

Duff I once knew a chap called Bleaker. He was at Roby's with me. Nice chap. Slight speech impediment. Nothing much. Very good at rugby and a useful change bowler. Married a laboratory assistant.

Stephen Sounds a pretty average sort of chap.

Duff Except that he sweated more than any man I've ever known. He was a prop forward. I used to rub up against him during scrum downs. It was like trying to grab hold of the Aswan Dam.

Stephen Poor blighter . . .

Duff Well, it was all right during rugby – we were *all* dripping by the end – but old Bleaker used to sweat at *functions*. Even on quite cool days, he was always dabbing himself with a handkerchief.

Stephen (*taps paper*) Well his perspiration glands were secreting in direct relation to his body temperature, you see. The chap would have probably boiled over if it hadn't been for his perspiration glands.

Duff Yes, I suppose so. Anyway he got married . . . had endless kids, so I don't suppose it . . .er . . .

Stephen No, I don't think it affects all that.

Pause.

Duff Took old Nelson to have his balls done yesterday. That's why he's making such a din! I'm just taking him for a walk to get his mind off it.

Virginia *enters.*

Virginia Hello, Duff . . . creeping in the back way?

Duff Hello Ginny . . . no, I was just taking Nelson for a walk, thought I'd drop in . . .

Stephen He's had his balls off.

Virginia (*momentarily thrown, but recovering*) . . . Oh . . . ?

Duff (*embarrassed*) . . . Well you know, whatever they do with dogs. Just took him down yesterday.

Virginia Much safer I'm sure . . .

Stephen She was always on at me to have a vasectomy . . .

Virginia Don't be silly dear.

Stephen Of course, that was before the condom revolution. You can hardly find a shop nowadays that *doesn't* sell the bloody things. They'll be dishing them out in church next. Decorating the altar with them at Harvest Festival. What about you Duff? Have you ever availed yourself of the services of a vasectomist?

Duff Hardly worth it at my age old bean.

Stephen Yes, I suppose you're pretty much out of trouble –

Virginia Really darling! Would you like some coffee, Duff . . . ?

Duff Only if you're making it Ginny.

Virginia Oh, there's some in the pot, it's no trouble . . . (*She bustles off.*)

Stephen (*shouting after her*) Get him a beer!

Duff (*looking after* **Virginia**, *but not significantly*) It's supposed not to make any difference to your sexual drive anyway . . .

Stephen Depends what sort of car you've got . . . (**Stephen** *laughs. Alone.*)

Duff No, you know what I mean . . . it doesn't affect the libido. And they can do it in ten minutes.

Stephen Really, it takes me anything up to an hour these days.

Duff No . . . the operation.

Stephen Virginia usually reads for the first forty-five minutes. Does the household accounts, that sort of thing.

There is a pause. **Duff** *appears to be wanting to say something.*

Duff You know . . . Bridget and I are at it rather a lot these days. Ever since she had her new hairstyle.

Stephen Looks better does she?

Duff Yes . . . yes . . . she looks much better, she seems a lot more . . . confident with herself . . .

Stephen Really? You surprise me.

Duff (*ignoring this*) Something in her general bearing. She wears brighter colours and she's always singing to herself and she's terribly nice to me . . .

Virginia *enters singing to herself and carrying* **Duff**'s *cup of coffee.*

Virginia Do you take sugar Duff dear . . . ? I can never remember.

Duff Oh thank you Ginny . . . you are kind . . .

Stephen *stops whatever he was going to say, and looks at his wife for a moment.*

Virginia, *brightly, pulls a little table across to* **Duff**'s *armchair and puts his cup down carefully.*

Duff No. No sugar thank you . . . I have these (*He feels in his pocket and waves a tin of Hermesetas.*) . . . keeps the old waistline down . . .

Virginia Oh yes, lots of people use them these days . . .

Stephen Oh yes, lots . . . I think they're especially popular in Ethiopia.

Virginia Well I'll leave you two to natter . . . I must go and stock up for tomorrow.

Duff Full house this weekend?

Virginia Yes . . . Alan and Diana and the children are coming . . .

Duff Oh, that'll be nice.

Music . . .

Fade to black. And slowly fade up again.

The television is on. It's evening. **Stephen** *sits in his armchair watching intently. The television set has its back to the audience.* **Virginia** *is at a writing desk behind him. Pause for some while, as we take all this in.*

Television But although the male mantis can now begin to mate, (*The voice is unmistakably Attenburian*) the female still clasps him in her wickedly barbed arms. As they copulate, she slowly begins to eat him.

That's his head gone.

Munching noises. Music. **Stephen** *reacts with brow furrowed in concentration.*

Headless though he may be, his abdomen continues to pulse, jetting sperm into her. (*Film sound. More mantis passion.*) The male dragonfly, on the other hand, has a better time of it. His penis is equipped with a bristling armoury of spines at the tip . . .

Stephen *gets up rather crossly.*

. . . with which he cleans out the female's tract . . .

He switches off the set.

Stephen (*to himself*) Filth!

He stands for a moment indecisively, then moves over to the sideboard. He pauses in front of it, then with well-practised skill begins to open a door and silently extricate a bottle of scotch. He has the scotch halfway up when **Virginia**, *with equally practised skill, addresses him without even turning.*

Virginia Are you having another?

Stephen No . . . no . . . I'm just getting the bottle out to check the spelling on the label.

Virginia Well, just have a small one. It's nearly bedtime.

Stephen Darling, when do you ever see me having anything other than small ones? We bought this bottle when George the Sixth was alive and it's still over half full.

Virginia I don't like to see you boozing all the time, that's all dear . . .

Stephen Boozing! Me! . . . *Boozing.* I've had two tiny whiskies today . . .

Virginia And some wine . . .

Stephen Oh, wine . . . yes, *lots* of wine. One glass of red with –

Virginia Two . . .

Stephen Two tiny glasses of red with the meal . . . That's not boozing. Do you realise that the per . . .

Virginia (*she's heard all this so often, she knows it by heart*) . . . capita consumption of the average Frenchman is two hundred bottles a year . . . yes, I know all that darling . . . but . . . well you know. I don't want you to end up like Cyril Toshack . . .

Stephen Listen, Cyril Toshack was an alcoholic. Cyril Toshack drank more before breakfast than I have in a *week* – (*Sotto voce.*) lucky bugger . . . I cannot 'end up' like Cyril Toshack. I *have* ended up . . . and I am *not* like Cyril Toshack!

Virginia All right.

Stephen (*with exaggerated courtesy*) Thank you . . .

Stephen *unscrews the cap, and pulls a glass over. He pours. Then pulls another glass over and pours again.*

(*With well-practised deference.*) One for *you* dear?

Virginia No! Of course not.

Stephen Just asking!

With a slight smile of satisfaction he pours **Virginia***'s whisky swiftly into his own glass.*

(*Walking back to his chair.*) What are you doing?

Virginia Writing . . .

Stephen Who to?

Virginia Marjorie's brother.

Stephen Oh that one-eyed old pervert . . .

Virginia He has perfectly good eyes dear . . .

Stephen In a box.

Virginia I don't think you can really chastise a man for losing an eye. He was serving his country at the time . . .

Stephen He's such an incompetent fart, he probably stuck his binoculars in too far.

Virginia If that's what whisky does for you . . .

Stephen Well I don't like her and I don't like him. And I don't like all that war hero stuff. Just because he rounded up a couple of Mau Mau doesn't give him a God-given right to be superior. I mean Duff isn't like that and he was parachuted into Suez.

Fought the Gippos single-handed till those traitorous American bastards pulled us out.

Pause. **Stephen** *drinks.*

You know Duff was telling me today that he and Bridget are always at it . . .

Virginia Quarrelling?

Stephen No, the opposite . . . you know . . . in bed . . .

Virginia Bridget's always at it, I'm not so sure about Duff . . .

Stephen What do you mean?

Virginia (*a slight pause, but she goes on writing*) . . . It's all over the village . . .

Stephen What do you mean, Virginia?

Virginia What do you mean, what do I mean?

Stephen What's all over the village . . . ?

Virginia That Bridget's having an affair . . .

Stephen Bridget?

Virginia Yes, Bridget . . .

Stephen *Duff's* Bridget . . . ?

Virginia (*with a little irritation*) . . . Yes . . .

Stephen Who with?

Virginia A foot specialist up in London.

Stephen But . . . But . . . she's so amazingly unattractive.

Virginia Not to everyone dear.

Stephen *is now truly grabbed.*

Stephen How do you know?

Virginia Marjorie saw her with him in Harrods . . .

Stephen Well that's not a crime . . .

Virginia They were buying sheets.

Stephen How do you know he's a foot specialist . . . ?

Virginia Well you know she had all that trouble last year with her feet . . .

Stephen No . . .

Virginia Well, she did . . . and Duff advised her to go to a specialist and er . . . it all sort of happened.

Stephen What do you mean . . . 'it sort of happened' . . . ?

Virginia The appointments began to get longer . . . two or three days sometimes.

Stephen So . . . ?

Virginia Oh use your imagination! There's a limit to the amount you can do with someone's feet!

Stephen Well . . . (*Pause. He walks to the sideboard and stands poised.*) . . . Well . . . what a bitch. To do something like that to old Duff.

Stephen *reaches to open the cupboard.*

Virginia Well, it's time for bed . . . busy day tomorrow.

She licks the envelope she's been writing and stamps it with a brisk air of finality. She get up and crosses to the door.

Stephen What's he like, this foot specialist . . . ?

Virginia Oh . . . I don't know. What are foot specialists normally like?

Stephen Well, is he young, old . . . married . . . half Namibian?

Virginia I've never seen him. Marjorie saw him.

Stephen And did she venture any description?

Virginia Middle-aged. Fair hair.

Stephen Oh that's brilliant. I can't imagine why Marjorie ever left MI5.

Virginia Will you do Alaric? (*She disappears into the kitchen.*)

Stephen Isn't he in?

Virginia (*off*) No he's been out since breakfast . . .

Stephen (*goes into kitchen. Off*) Does Bridget ever talk to you about this foot specialist . . . ?

Virginia *comes out of the kitchen with a bowl of flowers.* **Stephen** *follows, rather dog-like.*

Virginia No, of course not. (*She puts the vase outside on the patio.*) . . . There . . . I think those look much nicer there.

Stephen I preferred them in the kitchen.

Virginia We can't have them in the kitchen at the weekend.

Stephen Why not . . . ?

Virginia Because of Charlotte. You know she's allergic to things like that.

Stephen She's allergic to life.

Virginia Don't be silly dear. It's not a pleasant thing . . .

Stephen No one was allergic when I was a boy. If I'd told my father that I was allergic to leaf mould he'd have smacked me in the teeth.

Virginia (*as she briskly picks up some knitting and puts it away*) Which is why you are what you are dear.

Stephen What do you mean by that?

Virginia You know what I mean . . .

She goes to the hallway door.

Stephen *follows, trying to manoeuvre himself into a good position for a verbal coup-de-grâce.*

Stephen Perhaps you ought to go and get yourself a foot specialist.

Virginia Perhaps I will!

She exits briskly.

The lights fade leaving **Stephen** *in a spotlight.*

We hear the doorbell go. **Stephen** *turns his head to the sound. A door opens. He hears the following exchange between his wife and a smoothly powerful male voice:*

Smooth male Good evening, I'm a very distinguished foot specialist.

Virginia . . . Oh . . . how nice . . .

Smooth male Slip your things off would you?

Virginia But it's only the right foot.

Smooth male Let *me* be the judge of that, Mrs Febble . . .

Virginia Please call me Virginia.

Smooth male Virginia . . .

Virginia (*catching a breath*) Oh . . .

Smooth male (*medically*) Ah!

Virginia Oh . . .

Smooth male (*diagnosis established*) Mm . . .

Virginia (*eagerly*) Yes?

Smooth male Left fifth . . .

Virginia Yes?

Smooth male There's pressure . . .

Virginia . . . Oh yes . . .

Smooth male That must be relieved . . .

Virginia Yes . . . yes . . .

Smooth male Change your footwear . . .

Virginia Oh yes . . .

Smooth male Use these cornplasters.

Virginia Yes! . . . Yes! . . . Yes!

Smooth male And come and see me in a week.

Virginia (*a final, orgasmic cry*) Oh . . . YES!

A champagne cork pops. Romantic music soars, and climaxes. Silence.

Back in real time **Virginia***'s shout brings* **Stephen** *out of his increasingly agitated reverie.*

Virginia Stephen!

Lights up. **Virginia** *puts her head round the door.*

(*Briskly.*) Stephen, please will you do Alaric . . . It's going to be a busy day tomorrow.

Stephen (*jerked back to the present, which he greets with irritation*) Yes . . . yes . . . all right . . . bloody weekends.

Stephen *crosses to the french windows, opens one and shouts into the night.*

Alaric! Al . . . ar . . . ic! . . . Ricky! . . .Ricky . . . ticky . . . tooooo. (*He goes out onto the patio.*) Come on . . . Come on . . . Alaric . . . Who's a good little pussy? . . . *Who's* a good little pussy . . . Alaric . . . you little bastard!! . . .

Saturday

Fade lights up on breakfast, the next morning. **Stephen**, *looking morose, and* **Virginia** *drink tea in silence.*

Stephen Maybe the A57 will have been mined by the Iraqis.

Virginia They don't come that way now, they come down the A1(M). It cuts an hour off the journey. Diana says . . .

Stephen Oh my God . . . does the Ministry of Transport ever stop to think what misery its Motorway Programme inflicts on people . . .

Virginia She is your daughter.

Stephen It's so bloody disruptive.

Virginia It's nice to have people in the house occasionally!

Stephen We *always* have people in the house . . . it's either that Red charwoman . . .

Virginia (*correcting briskly*) Cleaning lady dear . . .

Stephen Or Marjorie with her –

Virginia Don't start about Marjorie . . .

Stephen We never have any time to just sit and talk . . .

Virginia Talk about what, dear?

Stephen Well . . . all sorts of things . . .

Virginia Like what . . . ?

Stephen Well . . . like all that business you were telling me about Bridget.

Virginia Oh . . . that . . .

Stephen Well don't sound so bloody dismissive. When you hear your best friend's wife is running around with another man . . . you sort of well . . . it starts you thinking . . .

Virginia I don't think it's anything we can interfere in, dear. And anyway, a lot of it's gossip, you know . . . I really don't know how far it's got.

Stephen No, it just made me think that's all . . .

Virginia Well don't for heaven's sake go telling Duff if that's what you're thinking . . .

Stephen No, it was nothing to do with Duff. It was . . . well it made me think that perhaps – you and I . . . er . . .

Bell goes.

Virginia Oh no . . . it can't be them already . . . Perhaps it is . . . Diana said they might leave early . . . Oh good heavens . . . (*She rushes to the door, undoing her apron.*) It *is* them!

Sound of front door opening. Confused rush of greetings. Noise of kissings, dogs, children.

Stephen *picks up the knife from his plate and passes it suicidally across his throat.*

Voices off.

Virginia And Emma couldn't get away . . . ? Oh what a shame . . . so you just brought Charlotte . . . Oh well it's lovely to see you and so early . . . it'll mean you'll have a really good long day.

Alan Down Pippa down (*Noise of barking.*) . . . Oh look she's gone straight upstairs . . . onto Grandad's bed – that's her favourite spot.

Stephen *leaps up at this, clutching the knife. He's like that when* **Virginia** *leads them in.*

Charlotte (*a fifteen-year-old girl, in modern teenage attire*) Hello Grandad . . .

She runs round and gives him an awkward peck on the cheek, before flinging herself down on the sofa and opening a book. **Stephen** *looks bleakly down at her.*

Alan, *a very boring thirty-eight-year-old with a moustache and receding hair, and* **Diana**, *the* **Febbles**' *thirty-two-year-old daughter, enter. Both are holding bags and baskets, and* **Alan** *is holding a Jokari set. Their appearance gives* **Stephen** *much pain.*

Alan Hello Grandad . . .

Diana Hello Daddy . . .

Diana's *less than cheerful greeting sounds worse as she looks at the knife.* **Stephen**, *suddenly aware he's holding it murderously, lowers it quickly.*

Stephen (*kissing her briefly*) Why are you so early?

Alan Marvellous journey. B6097, onto the A633 to Conisborough. A630 Doncaster road right through to the A1, then it's motorway almost down to Worksop and good dual as far as the A45. Bit of resurfacing at Brampton so we picked up the B1040 at Fenstanton, clear down the A45 which is dualled right the way through to Stowmarket. Good old 1120 to Saxtead, B1119 and home. Three hours fifty-seven minutes. Twenty-three and a half faster than we ever managed in the Cavalier.

Virginia *enters again busily.*

Virginia Well, I expect you'd like some breakfast, whatever time did you have to get up . . . ?

Diana Alan set the organiser for 5.45!

Stephen (*irritably*) Organiser?

Alan Yes the IQ 9000, Personal Organiser . . . got it in Hamburg. It's a memory-expandable time information management system.

Stephen Will someone tell me what he's talking about?

Virginia Oh that sounds marvellous . . . coffee or tea?

Alan You can set your own database or use a built-in calendar application that can tell you at a glance all your appointments for the next six days.

Stephen God alive . . .

Alan . . . How many days to the next dental check-up. Instant calculation of property depreciation after fixed rate for insurance . . .

Virginia How many for toast?

Alan Yes, it'd probably tell you that.

Virginia (*missing* **Alan***'s drift completely*) Are you going to eat the other bit Stephen . . . ?

Stephen (*quickly, possessively*) Yes . . . all the other bits.

Virginia I'll put some more in then . . .

She goes.

Alan (*to* **Charlotte**) Come on Charlotte, get your head out of that book, you've only just arrived.

Stephen *picks up some toast and very deliberately spreads it whilst reading the paper.* **Charlotte** *puts down her book reluctantly. She stares at* **Stephen** *for a while. Then does a very loud stage whisper to* **Diana**.

Charlotte Grandpa's not shaved . . .

Diana (*whispering back*) Ssh! He's only just got up.

Charlotte Is he in some sort of emotional trouble?

Diana Don't be silly . . .

Charlotte That's how people look on *Brookside* when they're in terrible emotional trouble . . .

Virginia *re-enters.*

Virginia Tea or coffee?

Alan Tea . . . for me please.

Diana Have you any decaffeinated . . . ?

Virginia Well I've just got the ordinary coffee dear, but there's a bit of real at the back of one of the cupboards . . .

Diana No, it's all right . . . I'll have some lemon tea, if there's no decaffeinated . . .

Stephen (*not looking up from his paper*) . . . Sake for me please . . .

Charlotte What's sake . . . ?

Virginia Just his little joke . . .

She goes to the kitchen. **Diana** *follows.*

Alan Sake's Japanese darling . . . it's a Japanese drink. They give you sake on all the Japan Airlines flights. Have you ever had sake Grandad?

Stephen Yes we used to drink it all the time in the war. It's all they'd give us on the Burma Road. Every time you built a station they'd give you a cup of sake.

Alan (*a little impressed*) You weren't on the Burma Road were you Grandad . . . ?

Stephen No . . . no . . . I wasn't actually. Didn't go to the right school.

Charlotte You'd only have been twelve.

Stephen Thank you, Mastermind. As a matter of fact I served my country from 1949 to 1951. In other theatres of war.

Charlotte Where did you serve?

Stephen Behind the lines.

Charlotte Where?

Stephen Northampton.

Charlotte The war was in Korea.

Stephen How do you know that?

Charlotte We're doing it for Special Studies – war and the myth of Empire.

Stephen The *myth* of Empire . . . I tell you my girl, if any one of those pansy teachers of yours had been fit to hold a candle to those men –

Charlotte What did you do?

Stephen I was proud to serve in His Majesty's Royal Army Pay Corps.

Charlotte You paid people to kill other people?

Stephen We paid people whatever was necessary to preserve freedom, decency and democracy.

Charlotte And the Empire . . .

Stephen Listen, Miss Trotsky – there wasn't so much wrong with the bloody Empire. Look at the way the world's falling apart now. Is that any better?

Charlotte At least they're free . . .

Stephen Well at least they don't have to learn the history of *their* country from some pinko vegan with a degree from North Bootle Technical College.

Alan No, it's the University of Merseyside now, isn't it?

Charlotte Eurrggghhhh!

Stephen *is distracted from a stinging riposte.*

Charlotte (*she points in revulsion at a bowl on the table*) What are *those*?

Stephen Figs.

Charlotte D'you eat them . . . ?

Stephen No, I use them as bathplugs . . .

Alan You've seen figs before dear . . .

Charlotte Not like that . . .

Stephen *retreats behind his paper again.* **Charlotte** *goes over to* **Alan** *and whispers loudly.*

Charlotte Aren't they for people who can't . . .

Alan Ssh! Go and help your granny.

Charlotte (*leaving slowly, gazing back at the figs with fascinated revulsion*) Eurgghh . . . they look so . . . so naked.

She goes.

Stephen Amazing the words they know at their age.

Alan Oh yes . . . times have certainly changed . . .

Stephen Did you read that somewhere or was it just off the top of your head?

Alan (*missing the irony by several lengths*) Oh, I think it's a fairly common sort of phrase. You hear it more and more these days, though.

Stephen Yes . . . there was a whole evening devoted to it on Radio 4 the other night. Fourteen solid hours with a break in between for some light music.

Alan What? Just about that one phrase . . . ?

Stephen (*getting up*) Well, I must go and dress . . .

Alan Talking of Radio 4 did you hear that very good programme on containerisation on Sunday?

Stephen No . . . no . . . I missed it for some reason. I think I was probably folding paper bags at the time . . .

Alan It was very interesting . . .

Stephen Really? What sort of thing was it . . . ? Lauren Bacall and Frank Sinatra reminiscing about container ports. Leonardo da Vinci's recently discovered sketches for a roll-on, roll-off easy access bulk food transport system?

Alan No, it was all about these plans to put a six-lane access road through here.

Stephen Through *here*?

Alan Well, through Canfield . . . to connect the B1353 and the old A12 at –

Stephen Canfield . . . you mean *our* Canfield?

Alan Canfield, Suffolk . . . yes, there was quite a lot about this area.

Stephen When . . . ?

Alan When what?

Stephen When did you hear this?

Alan After *Your Hundred Best Tunes* . . . I was listening because the firm is considering an exploratory survey of bulk cargo techniques . . .

Virginia *passes through with some flowers.*

Virginia Aren't these lovely!

Stephen Did you hear anything about this road through Canfield?

Virginia What dear?

Stephen Some nonsense about a six-lane access road through the village.

Virginia Oh . . . you mean the container development . . .

Stephen What container development . . . ?

Virginia At Thorpeness . . .

Alan That's it . . . Thorpeness . . .

Stephen I never heard about any container development at Thorpeness.

Virginia *selects a vase and tries out the flowers in it.*

Virginia (*vaguely*) Oh, there's been talk of it for years.

Stephen Duff's never mentioned it . . .

Virginia Well, Duff wouldn't.

Charlotte (*shouts from kitchen*) Kettle's boiled Granny . . .

Virginia All right . . . darling . . . I'm coming . . .

She disappears into the kitchen.

Stephen What do you mean by that . . . ?

He follows her into the kitchen. As he goes in she comes out, busily, with a tray of freshly made coffee and some teacups and saucers.

Virginia Don't be so dense dear. You know Duff's on the Rural District . . . they could hardly go ahead without him knowing . . . could you bring the cups.

Stephen He's never said a word to me.

Virginia Well why should he dear? Move those plates would you Charlotte . . . ?

Virginia *stands with the tray poised waiting for the table to be cleared.*

Alan Containerisation is the way it's going . . .

Stephen (*to* **Virginia**, *who is having some difficulty holding the tray*) . . . Mmm?

Virginia What dear?

Stephen Why would Duff not have told me?

Alan Do you know that when they build the deep-water terminal at Rotterdam this coast could see a ninety-four per cent increase in container activity?

Stephen (*still to* **Virginia**) We're supposed to be friends.

Virginia (*going to the door and shouting*) Di . . . I've made your tea . . . !

Diana (*off*) Yes I'm coming. Pippa's just made a mess . . .

Virginia Oh no . . .

Stephen Listen if Duff had heard anything about six-lane motorways he'd have told me.

Virginia Alan, help yourself to tea, I won't be a moment . . . (*She goes to the door of the hall and calls up to* **Diana**.) Bucket or newspaper?

Diana (*calling down*) Bucket *and* newspaper!

Virginia *makes to go to the kitchen.*

Alan I'll do it Virginia.

Alan *goes into the kitchen after the bucket.* **Stephen** *retreats behind his paper.*

Virginia Well why don't you go and *see* him and ask him . . . ?

Stephen Why should I?

Virginia Because you want to know . . .

Diana *runs in and goes to the kitchen.*

Stephen It's up to him. I don't see why I should have to go scampering round there just because he won't tell me.

Virginia Well, don't sit there and mope about it . . .

Stephen I'm not sitting and moping, I'm reading the paper.

Diana (*grabbing a newspaper, makes for the door*) You're the only person I know who has to memorise the *Daily Telegraph*!

Alan *follows with the bucket,* **Charlotte** *with a mop.*

Stephen Just because I choose to be well informed, unlike certain members of this family.

He puts the paper up again having delivered this barb. The little clearing procession – **Diana**, **Alan**, **Charlotte** *– exit.* **Virginia** *closes the door. There is an unrelaxed silence.*

Virginia Did you know that Di and Alan may be separating?

Stephen What . . . ?

Virginia She just mentioned it this morning. Out of the blue. When we were in the kitchen.

Stephen What!

Virginia Anyway, don't say anything. She'll bring it up no doubt.

She goes to the kitchen. **Stephen** *lowers his paper slowly as he takes in this fresh bombshell. For a moment or two even he is silenced. Then he rises quite sharply and heads for the kitchen.*

Stephen If the Third World War breaks out while I'm on the lavatory, could someone bang on the door . . . !

Fade.

Fade up.

Later in the morning. A game of Scrabble is in progress. Playing are all except **Virginia**, *who inconspicuously but persistently bustles away, clearing, tidying, preparing. She often goes out to the kitchen and we hear her running water, opening and shutting cupboards etc., all carefully orchestrated to be just distracting at the right moments.*

Diana It's not very inspired, but if you could see the letters I've got . . .

Charlotte I can . . .

Diana What?

Charlotte See the letters you've got . . .

Diana Well, don't look. (*She moves her letter rack round.*)

Alan Grandad can see them now . . .

Diana Oh! . . . there . . . (*She gets the letter rack positioned and unloads a word onto the board.*)

Alan Eel.

Charlotte That's good Mum . . .

Stephen *raises his eyes a fraction at this.*

Diana Double letter score on the 'L'.

Stephen (*damply*) Four.

Charlotte What are the scores . . . ?

Alan Er . . . well . . . your mother's got fifty-six, you've got one hundred and two, I've got ninety and (*Quickly.*) Grandfather's got thirty-one.

Stephen Just because you wouldn't let me have 'ex-quin' . . .

Charlotte There was no such word.

Diana Oh don't start that again, darling.

Stephen 'Ex-quin'. Someone who *used* to be a quin.

Charlotte It's not in the dictionary . . .

Stephen Not in the dictionary *we're* using . . .

Charlotte It's the *Shorter Oxford*, Grandpa . . . it's in two volumes.

Stephen Listen, *The* Oxford Dictionary has thirteen volumes. Now when you're talking about dictionaries, *that* is a dictionary . . . that probably has eight pages on 'ex-quin' alone!

Diana It's your go, Dad . . .

Stephen I'm about to go, thank you. All I'm saying is that the scoring is fairly academic as I would and indeed should, if we had a decent set of dictionaries, be up to one hundred and ninety-six.

Virginia Lunch'll be ready in about ten minutes . . .

Charlotte Ooh good should be finished by then . . .

Stephen, *staring bleakly at his letters, shoots her a glance. There is a long silence as* **Stephen** *rearranges his letters.* **Diana** *lights a cigarette.* **Virginia**, *with only a momentary pause, disappears busily into the kitchen, and reappears with a small ashtray which she slips onto the table beside her daughter.*

Virginia Sorry dear, I thought you'd given up, so I'd put them all away . . .

Diana I have one occasionally . . .

Virginia Of course dear. (*She can't help herself looking at* **Alan**. *He looks up from his rack and coughs loudly in* **Diana**'s *direction.*)

Virginia *goes back to setting out lunch on the main table. There is a noise of plates, small knives and other clattery objects, as the Scrabble players morosely wait for* **Stephen**. *After some moments* **Stephen** *suddenly looks up and rounds on* **Virginia**.

Stephen Do you *have* to do all that . . . ?

Virginia I'm only getting lunch.

Stephen Yes, but do you have to get it like that. It's terribly hard to concentrate with all that clatter. It's like the bazaar in Bonga-Bonga . . .

Virginia Well I'll go and finish off in the kitchen . . .

Stephen Why don't you just sit down, put your feet up and read the *Telegraph* for a bit . . .

Virginia And who'd get the meals if I *did*?

Stephen Oh . . . Mahatma Gandhi . . .

Diana *gives a short laugh.* **Alan** *brightens suddenly as if a good idea has just occurred to him. He calls to* **Virginia**.

Alan D'you want a hand?

Virginia No, for heaven's sake . . . you stay there and enjoy yourself . . .

Alan's *face drops.*

. . . I'll go and get quietly on in the kitchen.

She disappears. **Alan**'s *heavily orchestrated coughing has caused* **Diana** *to stub her cigarette out, with irritation. Silence falls again.* **Stephen** *juggles more letters, then stares at them. The rivetingly audible sounds of someone trying to get on with their activities as silently as possible emanate from the kitchen and should give the audience a laugh or two.*

Stephen (*after some deliberation*) Is there such a word as 'ig' . . . ?

Charlotte *Ig* . . . ?

Diana I don't think so, no . . .

Alan No, not as far as I know . . .

Stephen I'm sure there is. I think it's the word from which the diminutive 'igloo' is derived. 'Ig', I think you'll find, is a large Eskimo hall, and igloos are the small individual dwellings.

With a resigned but habitual gesture, **Charlotte** *passes the dictionary to* **Alan** *who passes it on to* **Stephen**.

Stephen (*flicking through*) . . . Ig . . . ig . . . ig . . . ig . . .

Diana There's no such word, Dad . . . come on . . .

Stephen (*rather smugly*) That's what you said about 'ugh'. (*He reaches the page and runs his finger down.*) . . . Bloody useless dictionary . . . ah . . . no hang on . . . here's an even better one . . . (*Looks at the letter rack and then back to the dictionary.*) . . . Yes . . . this is the one I was thinking of . . . (*He lays the letters down on the board.*)

Diana What's the blank?

Stephen 'G' . . . !

Diana 'Igbo' . . . ?

Stephen (*triumphantly smug*) . . . That's it . . .

Charlotte '*Igbo*'?

Stephen (*taps dictionary*) 'Variation of Ibo . . .' One . . . two, three, four, five, six . . . seven, double word score . . . fourteen and 'so' is two that's –

Charlotte What's an ibo?

Stephen Ibo! What's an Ibo? What do they teach you at your school? Ibo, or 'Igbo' as it can be known, is the language and the tribe of Northern Nigeria.

Alan It's a proper name though isn't it?

Stephen *turns on* **Alan** *who looks a little uncomfortable.*

Stephen It's a perfectly acceptable, normal, sound, legitimate noun . . . like 'spoon' or 'radish' or (*He fixes* **Alan** *with a look just above the right temple.*) . . . axe.

Alan Proper noun though isn't it . . . like British or Russian or . . . er Hovis . . .

Stephen (*dramatically*) Oh . . . well if you're going to start equating Hovis and Igbo.

Charlotte (*reading from dictionary*) Ibo . . . noun . . . Member or language of a Negro people of South-East Nigeria . . . brackets . . . native name . . .

Stephen There you are . . . native name . . . just like the native name for a tree or a stone . . . Nothing there about it being a *proper* noun . . .

He looks challengingly at **Alan** *but is outflanked by* **Charlotte.**

Charlotte If it's a native name then it's a foreign word . . .

Stephen So?

Charlotte Well you can't have proper nouns or foreign words . . .

Stephen Where does that put 'meringue' . . . ?

Virginia (*from the kitchen*) Coming dear!

Stephen . . . or 'chassis' . . . or 'guerrilla'? (*He looks around smugly.*) . . . foreign words all – which have passed into and enriched our native language, and a damn good thing too . . .

(*He rests like a barrister who has just made his most telling point after a four-hour summing up.*)

Diana 'Igbo' hasn't passed into the language . . .

Stephen Diana . . . how many books have you read . . . how often do you go to the theatre, how many newspapers do you take in the morning . . .?

Diana Oh! (*She turns away in exasperation and heads for the kitchen.*) . . . I'm going to help Mummy.

Alan (*getting up*) . . . No, let me.

Stephen Just because *Good Housekeeping* doesn't have an Igbo culture page . . . I suppose that makes it forbidden.

Diana and **Alan** *have gone into the kitchen.*

Stephen (*shouting after them*) It's like playing with the bloody Pope!

Charlotte I'll let you have 'Igbo' . . .

Stephen I should think so too. (*He pulls the scoring pad over from* **Alan***'s place.*) . . . Sixteen . . . (*He writes.*)

Charlotte *lays out a series of letters ending on the triple word score.*

Stephen 'Zeugma'?

Charlotte It's a figure of speech . . . like when you use one verb or adjective to cover two nouns one of which it isn't strictly applicable to.

Stephen (*recovering*) I know . . . I know . . .

Charlotte . . . that's twenty-three and triple word score . . . sixty-nine . . . add 'areal' . . . that's down there . . . sixty-nine . . . eighty-four . . . that makes me one hundred and eighty-six and you're up to . . . forty-seven . . .

Stephen So . . . it's between you and me . . .

Suddenly there is a cacophony of fierce yapping out in the garden, and a few muffled human shouts of admonition.

Virginia (*banging on the kitchen window*) Nelson!

Charlotte *jumps up and races out to the garden,* **Virginia** *appears from the kitchen with a bowl of salad and runs out after her.* **Alan** *and* **Diana** *follow at a run.*

Strangely **Stephen** *appears not to notice. He pulls across the dictionary and thumbs through it keenly, glancing occasionally at his letters, his eyes agleam. He mouths odd bits of words.*

From outside we hear alternate vehement shouts from **Charlotte,** **Virginia** *and another voice we recognise . . .* **Duff.**

Voices Pippa! . . . Nelson! . . . Pippa . . . Nelson . . . Pippa! . . . NELSON!!!!

Finally the situation is calmed, the yelping ceases. A car door slams.

Duff's voice (*sternly*) Now stay in there!

Virginia *and* **Diana** *return . . .* **Virginia** *still holding the bowl of salad.*

Virginia He's only just been done . . . I'm sure the stitches are still in . . .

Diana Well . . . it was probably Pippa's fault, she's a terrible flirt . . .

Virginia It must hurt him *frightfully* . . . Stephen, have you finished the game?

Stephen Not by a long chalk.

Virginia Well could you put it away dear and we can all gather round and have a nice lunch.

Stephen Can't we have a nice lunch on a tray?

Virginia No.

Stephen Oh of course, I forgot it was one of those weekends when we all have to make a few sacrifices.

Virginia *sighs and grits her teeth.*

Diana (*as she helps lay the lunch table*) Was that Duff's dog?

Virginia That's right, Nelson . . . He's a dear dog really . . . but he has fathered an awful lot round here . . .

Diana Duff's so nice isn't he . . . Do you see much of him?

Virginia Oh, he pops in every now and then . . . They're coming round tonight . . .

Stephen (*he freezes*) What? *More* people are coming . . . Haven't we *enough*?

Virginia (*patiently*) There you see . . . you've forgotten already . . .

Stephen I haven't forgotten, I never knew!

Diana *exits to the garden.*

Virginia We asked Duff and Bridget to dinner three weeks ago . . . Of course you knew.

Stephen I *never* knew. I hate dinner parties. Especially on Saturday. I miss three good films! If you'd told me I would have *absolutely* vetoed it, or made arrangements to visit Thailand.

Virginia I *did* tell you. (*She starts to clear the table.*)

Stephen You never told me.

Virginia Yes I did . . . and I wrote it on the calendar in the kitchen.

Stephen Oh no you didn't. If you'd written it on the calendar I would know about it. I'm not a fool, I pass that every day . . .

There's a commotion at the french windows. More doggy yelps. **Alan**, **Diana** *and* **Charlotte** *enter.*

Diana (*clutching the dog*) . . . You're a very naughty girl, Pippa . . .

Stephen Oh look, do we *have* to have the beast in this house?

Diana She's been very naughty . . . she's torn up the candytuft.

Charlotte *moves over and takes her.*

Charlotte It's not Pippa's fault . . .

Stephen Was it that bloody candytuft again . . . attacking dogs . . . ?

Charlotte She was excited by that other dog . . .

Virginia Look! Put her upstairs dear, while we're having lunch.

Stephen Don't you dare!

Virginia In the spare room.

Stephen Leave her in the garden.

Virginia We can't leave her in the garden.

Stephen Tie her up.

Charlotte (*protectively, to the dog as much as to* **Stephen**) No, she didn't come here to be tied up did you . . . darling . . .

Stephen If the beast can't behave inside or out she should be tied up or left in the car.

Charlotte You're a Nazi.

Alan Charlotte!

Stephen So you're a world authority on Nazis now.

Virginia Lunch!

Stephen I tell you, if I were a Nazi, that dog would have been blotting paper long ago . . .

Virginia Lunch!

Charlotte They didn't like anyone weaker than themselves.

Virginia Diana, there are just the hot sausage rolls to bring in, dear . . .

Charlotte They were bullies like you.

Stephen Don't you dare speak to me like that you precocious little squirt . . . !

Virginia Now, Alan you're here . . . (*She stands over the table.*) Stephen . . . you can go at the end so you can serve the salad . . .

Stephen This country fought against the Nazis for six years, for your freedom.

Diana *appears with the hot sausage rolls.*

Virginia Diana . . . you're here next to . . . me.

Charlotte Freedom to tie my dog up . . . ?

Stephen There are *other* freedoms you know . . .

Virginia Come on you two stop arguing . . . it's lunchtime.

Stephen Freedom to have a clean tie or keep shit off the carpet, or grow candytuft . . . what about those freedoms?

Virginia Charlotte darling put Pippa up in the spare room over lunch.

Stephen With her bowel record? You must be mad.

Charlotte She's staying here with me . . . I can hold her.

Virginia You can't hold a dog and eat salad dear.

Stephen Either the dog goes or I go!

Virginia Go where . . . ?

Stephen Anywhere . . . anywhere where the dog is not. (*He rises.*) And preferably where that girl is not either.

He walks across the room and out of the hallway door. There is a silence for a while at the table. **Stephen** *reappears, walks to the table, grabs his lager and exits again. A door slams off.*

Diana Why do we come . . . ?

Virginia Because we love to see you dear . . .

Fade.

Fade up.

Early evening. The room has been tidied. The table is laid for dinner.

After a moment's pause to take in with anticipation and delight the pristine arena, the audience is treated to the sight of **Virginia**, *immaculately attired, entering from the hall. She smiles thoroughly and efficiently as she appraises the effect of her thoroughness and efficiency upon this well-ordered living room. She makes a last adjustment to the table – setting an ashtray for Diana.*

Then she stops. Her smile fades and is replaced by a look of troubled concern. She sniffs. She moves a little further from the table and sniffs again. Her olfactory curiosity leads her towards a rather fine, antique sideboard, probably the only expensive piece of furniture in the room. As she reaches it, her final sniff changes in mid-intake to a look of gasping horror. She bends down briefly and up again fast.

She has just registered the Thing that is down by the valuable sideboard when **Stephen** *enters. He wears a Marks and Spencer's cardigan over well-pressed grey trousers, an open-necked shirt and a cravat.*

Stephen (*who's obviously spent some time selecting this outfit*) Well . . . how's this?

Virginia (*anxious that he should not come any further towards the source of the offensive pong*) That's absolutely fine . . . Perhaps you'd better go and get the drinks ready . . .

Stephen You don't think I should wear the blazer . . . ?

Virginia Have you got the tonic waters yet . . . ?

Stephen I know this is the Age of Casual Leisurewear, but I always think this sort of stuff lacks smartness. (*He plucks at the M & S cardigan.*) It's neither one thing or the other. I mean this is like a sort of detumescent jacket.

Virginia Well . . . er . . . fine . . . perhaps you should wear the blazer . . .

Stephen On the other hand, I don't want to make it look as though I was the only one who went to Cambridge. Well, what do you think . . . ?

Virginia About what, dear?

Stephen About the jacket . . . ?

Virginia Whatever you feel most comfortable in dear . . .

Stephen I'd feel most comfortable watching television with my top three flies undone . . .

Virginia Stephen . . .

Stephen The point is what do I *have* to wear in order to avoid frightful social embarrassment all round.

Virginia Try the blazer, I'm sure it'll look nice!

Stephen *is about to speak, but then with a grunt of exasperated indecision, exits.* **Virginia** *takes a quick look out of the window to check the coast is clear and then crosses to the fireplace and picks up a small ornamental shovel. She crosses to the sideboard, bends down and gingerly tries to shovel up the mess. She can't quite manage it and looks round* *desperately. On the sideboard above her is a copy of the* Telegraph. *She grabs it and swiftly uses it to scrape the mess onto the shovel. She straightens up. She has not gone two paces when the front-door bell rings. She stands rooted to the spot.*

Virginia Oh, no . . . ! I said eight.

She looks around desperately for somewhere to lay the shit. She runs to the fireplace. Stops. The bell sounds again. She runs into the middle of the room, still holding the shit on the shovel. The bell rings again. **Stephen**, *wearing a blazer that is too small, races in.*

Stephen (*highly agitated*) I can't wear *this*!

Virginia (*desperately*) Answer the door!

Stephen What's that . . . ?

Virginia Dog mess . . .

Stephen What are you holding it for? There are people coming to dinner!

Virginia I *know* there are people coming to dinner, that's why I'm holding it!

Stephen (*picking at his blazer desperately*) Is it too small . . . ?

The bell goes.

Virginia (*goes to hallway door*) Diana!

Diana (*off*) I'm drying my hair!

Stephen *Is* it too *small*? . . . !

Virginia Get rid of it!

She thrusts the shovel into **Stephen**'s *hand . . . and exits through the kitchen.*

Virginia (*off*) Coming!

Sound of door opening . . . distant hellos. **Stephen**, *panic-stricken, turns, runs across to the mirror, looks at himself, decides that he does look ridiculous, turns, puts the shovel down on an elegant side table, and tears off his jacket. Voices are heard coming nearer.*

Duff (*off*) I thought it best to come a moment or two early to warn you . . .

Bridget (*off*) It's only *one* more . . .

Virginia (*off*) Oh . . . that's fine . . .

Another voice sounds in the hall.

Virginia (*off*) Oh good heavens, no . . . if we can't fit one more in . . . what . . . er . . . what *can* we do . . .

Stephen *has removed the jacket. In a blind panic as the voices get nearer, he loses his reason and stuffs the blazer behind the cushions on the sofa. He grabs the shit-bearing shovel and is about to whizz it out to the kitchen when the door opens. Desperately,* **Stephen** *deposits his malodorous burden on the nearest available surface – the dinner table.*

At that moment, the guests enter. **Bridget Gardner**, *a rather well-built, well-preserved ex-Roedean-type girl. She talks loudly in ringing, imperious upper-class tones. Behind her is* **Duff**. *Nice, warm, kindly* **Duff** *in a light grey suit with a regimental tie. Behind* **Duff** *and* **Bridget** *is the chiropodist* **Hugh Bedales**. *He looks pleasant, wears a slightly shapeless tweed jacket over flannels and smiles apologetically. He is much less oleaginous than he sounded in* **Stephen**'s *dream.*

Virginia Well . . . come through . . .

Stephen Hello! (*Forcing himself into a wholly unconvincing display of jollity*) . . . Hello Duff . . . Hello Bridget . . .

Bridget Hello Stephen . . .

She moves close to **Stephen** *and gives him a firm kiss. She glances down at his disarranged clothing.*

Bridget You're looking very 'alfresco' tonight . . .

Stephen *smiles weakly and tucks himself in.*

Bedales (*coming forward, hand extended*) And I'm the mystery guest. I *do* apologise . . .

Stephen, *horribly confused, grasps* **Bedales**' *hand.*

Bridget This is Hugh Bedales, Stephen . . .

Stephen (*uncomprehendingly*) Ah! How do you do . . .

Bridget Quite out of the blue rang our doorbell an hour ago . . .
on his way to a conference. I inveigled him round here despite
his protests . . . I knew you wouldn't mind . . . He does my feet.

Stephen *looks up sharply.* **Duff** *has started to sniff.* **Stephen** *registers
a momentary sharp twinge of horror as he remembers where he left the
shovel.*

Stephen Er . . . go in the garden!

Virginia Don't be silly dear.

Stephen Beautiful evening . . .

Bedales (*with interest*) The *garden* . . . ?

Stephen Oh yes . . . it's a lovely garden. Virginia's a genius
with small shrubs . . . I'll join you.

Duff *and* **Bedales** *wander out through the french windows, but*
Bridget *is hanging back admiringly.*

Bridget You're so frightfully *clever,* Ginny dear to be so
frightfully organised. It all looks lovely . . . Flowers from the
garden?

Virginia No, actually Diana and Alan –

Stephen (*desperately*) Yes! There are lots more outside.

He indicates the french windows, but neither **Bridget** *nor* **Virginia**
seems to be listening.

Bridget You're so good at colour. Everything *goes* so well . . .
The table and the candles and the – what's that?

Virginia, *who's been quickly tidying a couple of specks of dirt on the
mantelpiece, looks round.*

Virginia What's what . . . Bridget . . . ?

Bridget There's a shovel on the table with something nasty on
it . . . there, next to your super little Art Deco water jug.

Virginia *spins round, unsuccessfully suppressing a look of horror.*

Virginia Oh . . . that! That's Stephen . . .

Stephen What?

Bridget *gives a brief uncertain glance at* **Virginia**.

Bridget Stephen?

Virginia Look, do go into the garden, Bridget.

Virginia *picks it up hastily.*

Stephen left it there . . . Look . . .

She whips it off the table and marches out brandishing the shit on the shovel.

I've just got to put a few finishing touches to the cooking . . .

Bridget *looks confused.* **Stephen** *smiles horribly, his mouth working but very little sound coming out.*

Stephen (*eventually*) I like your hair . . .

The lights fade.

A few minutes later. **Stephen, Bridget, Bedales** *and* **Duff** *have been joined by* **Diana, Alan** *and* **Charlotte,** *in a fine punkish sort of outfit – bottle-green velour drainpipe trousers and a black loose-hanging top which reveals one shoulder alluringly. Lipstick and some green freckles around the nose. She is sitting on the side of her mother's chair rather sweetly sipping a dark gassy fluid and idly flicking through her magazine.* **Alan** *sits on a chair by the dinner table,* **Bridget, Bedales** *and* **Duff** *occupy the remaining comfortable chairs. They all have drinks. There is a long-enough-to-be-embarrassing silence for a moment after the lights come up. Then* **Bridget** *leans her head back and calls out behind her.*

Bridget (*stridently*) Anything I can do Ginny – ?

Virginia (*off*) No, I'm fine . . . you just enjoy yourselves!

Bridget *turns back to the silent room. There is a pause, then* **Stephen,** *as if suddenly attacked by an insect, leaps up into the silence.*

Stephen Another drink . . . Bridget . . . ?

Bridget Well, why not? Yes . . . I'll have a small one Stephen . . .

Stephen *furrows his brow enquiringly as he takes her glass.*

Bridget The usual . . .

Stephen (*confidently*) Right! (*He gets to the drinks table and obviously cannot remember.*) Campari and . . .

Bridget Gin and orange.

Stephen Gin and orange. Of course . . . yes . . . gin and orange.

Bridget And go easy on the gin this time, Stephen. I don't want to end up flat on my back.

General overpolite laughter.

Bedales A very good place to be . . .

No one's quite sure how to react to this. **Bedales** *smiles, a little apologetically.*

If we all spent more time flat on our backs, my life would be a lot easier.

Only **Alan** *laughs nervously here. Over by the sideboard* **Stephen** *is being a little noisy with the bottles.*

In my work . . . I see a great many feet every day. I see feet, crabbed and bent and swollen and misshapen, I see feet twisted and coiled with care, toes forced together in the name of high fashion.

Stephen *puts* **Bridget**'s *drink beside her and turns to* **Bedales**, *somewhat underestimating the impressive grip* **Bedales** *has established over his audience.*

Stephen Drink?

Bedales And the first thing I say to my patients – and this is the first thing I told Mrs Gardner – is lie down . . . lie down. Not on a couch or on a sofa, not on cushions or rugs . . . just lie down wherever you are.

He looks around, confidently assessing the impact of his words. **Stephen** *is behind him dumb-cramboing to* **Diana** *to find out what she wants to drink.*

And when they're lying down I ask them . . . how much time do you spend like this each day? How often do you lie flat out letting your back and your legs and your head take the weight which would otherwise be entirely or very largely thrown onto those poor, wretched, inadequate, overworked feet . . .

Diana *shakes her head and indicates a half-full glass.* **Stephen**
mouths . . . 'Alan . . . ?' **Alan** *nods and* **Stephen** *goes out to the fridge
in the kitchen.*

And the answer is perhaps seven, possibly eight or nine but
usually five or six hours in twenty-four. The rest of the time . . .
maybe eighteen hours, is spent moving around . . . journeys,
meetings, parties, conferences, and always . . . always it is the
feet . . . the feet who bear the brunt.

Tsst. As a beer can is opened behind him.

Charlotte Can I have some more Coke?

Diana (*who has perhaps been more genuinely impressed than anyone else
present*) Do you lie flat on the floor, Mr Bedales . . . ?

Bedales Oh indeed. I make a point of being prostrate at least
twice a day. Preferably naked.

Diana That sounds interesting.

Stephen Duff?

Duff Scotch please old boy . . .

Charlotte Why do you have to be naked?

Bridget (*quickly*) Have you driven down today Alan?

Alan Yes, marvellous journey.

Bedales Nakedness is the only honest way to display your body.

Alan Three hours fifty-seven minutes and that's with twenty-
eight miles of B-roads and a diversion at Brampton.

Bridget We have some friends in Whitby.

Bedales To regenerate, to revive, to free our true and
spontaneous feelings from the paraphernalia of repression.

Alan Yes, that's not far from us . . .

Bridget Lovely county, Yorkshire.

Alan Yes beautiful . . .

Diana But you can't expect people to walk around England with nothing on, specially in the winter . . .

Bridget I love York.

Alan Yes, very historical . . .

Bridget Terribly historical . . .

Bedales Go naked in the home . . . that's no great hardship. Two hours a day with nothing on will release forces within you which you never believed that you possessed.

Charlotte Eurghh!

Bridget Harrogate's very nice too . . .

Alan Not quite so historical – Harrogate . . .

Bedales Break the build-up of shame before it's begun . . .

Diana (*getting up*) I'm sure you're absolutely right . . . but this girl loves her clothes too much . . . Come on, time to take Pippa out.

Charlotte Why are you packing me off?

Diana I'm not packing you off, darling. I just want you to take Pippa for a walk . . . then you can have supper in Granny's room with the television.

Diana pushes her daughter towards the hall door.

Charlotte Can I come down later and see if you're all naked . . .?

Polite laughter. They exit. There is another pregnant silence.

Bridget Alan and Diana have come all the way down from Yorkshire . . .

Bedales Really?

Bridget Yes . . .

Bedales Well I never . . .

A pause.

Stephen Mr Bedales? A drink for you . . . ?

Bedales Do call me Hugh.

Stephen (*with exaggeration*) Hugh . . . a drink for you, Hugh?

Bedales No, I don't drink thank you. My father was an alcoholic for twenty years of his life. I've seen the ravages of that particular drug upon the body.

Stephen Mm . . . yes . . . er . . . Everybody else all right?

General nods.

(*Turning back to the drinks.*) Just me then . . . (*Aside to himself.*) For the ravages . . . (*He pours himself a generous whisky.*)

Bridget Have you been out in the garden today Stephen . . . ?

Stephen (*caught in mid-swig*) . . . Er . . . not a lot no . . . er . . . Virginia's the gardener really, I can't tell one end of a daffodil from the other.

Alan Funnily enough, there's a new garden centre near us on the A628 Dodworth road, just off the M1 Barnsley turn-off at Junction 37. Do you know they've built an entire slip-road just to join it up to the B6449?

Virginia *enters breezily. We will never know about the slip-road scandal.*

Virginia Well . . . it's ready at long last . . . Stephen would you like to get everyone sitting down . . . ? Stephen?

Stephen(*who hates this part of the dinner-party experience more than any other*) Ah . . . well . . .

Virginia Come on everybody.

They rise and move towards the table.

Stephen Duff and Bridget, you'd better sit on that side . . .

Virginia No . . . no, opposite dear . . .

Stephen Sorry . . . you and Duff opposite, and next to Duff is Alan . . .

Virginia (*correcting*) Diana.

Stephen Diana . . . Now let me see next to Diana is Hugh, so Alan had better be next to Bridget over there.

Virginia No . . . Hugh next to Bridget and Alan opposite . . .

Stephen Next to me . . .

Virginia No . . . no . . . you're next to Bridget and Duff . . .

Stephen Duff's up the other end . . .

Virginia No . . . no . . . Duff is . . .

Stephen *closes his eyes in utter despair.*

Stephen Oh God!

A flash of lightning. The group of people around the table are suffused with golden light from above. Celestial choirs are heard in soaring chorus. A deep and timeless voice rings out above them. They freeze.

Voice of the Lord Duff next to Diana opposite Alan. Hugh opposite Bridget next to Diana. Stephen between Hugh and Bridget. Mrs Febble between Duff and Alan.

Choirs crescendo. A final flash of lightning.

Curtain.

Act Two

A tremendous final flourish from on high. Shafts of heavenly light flash onto the dinner party. Then everything goes back to normal.

The guests un-freeze and seat themselves as instructed. **Virginia** *sees them settled and then goes out to the kitchen.*

Stephen *reaches for a bottle and approaches* **Bedales**.

Stephen (*to* **Bedales**) Do you take any wine . . . ?

Bedales No thank you Mr Febble . . . some mineral water if you have any . . . ?

Stephen (*with a certain satisfaction*) No, I'm afraid we don't have any mineral water. Will water without minerals do?

Bedales I'm sure that will be fine.

Stephen *lifts the water jug and pours rather purposely badly.*

Stephen It's just some old liquid out of the sky . . . I'm not exactly sure which part . . .

Bedales How kind . . . thank you . . .

Virginia *enters with a tray full of little dishes.*

Bridget Oh look . . . how *lovely* . . .

Virginia *puts the tray on the sideboard.*

Virginia Shrimp Surprise!

Bridget Oh, you're so clever!

Virginia Well wait till you've tasted it first . . . Pass them up could you Duff . . . to Diana . . .

Dishes are passed around and laid out.

It's rather good with this brown bread.

Stephen *moves round the table pouring liberal glassfuls of wine.*

Virginia *and* **Diana** *offer the bread around. Murmurs of thanks and appreciation. Eating begins.* **Virginia** *looks round with a quick harassed* *look of hostessy concern. Her eyes meet* **Stephen***'s for a moment, and she looks away, not happily. Perhaps she already senses that* **Stephen** *could be trouble, and despite her busy housewife and mother act she is aware too of the tensions within this group. But it has to be gone through, so she will try her best to supervise and guide the social proceedings with the same high standards of duty and service which she has applied to cooking, cleaning, and nursing of the mentally ill at the nearby Middleton Ridge hospital.*

Virginia Do you know this part of the world at all, Hugh?

Bedales Yes, as a matter of fact I do . . . I once had a boat at Woodbridge . . .

Virginia Oh really . . . ? That's a lovely spot . . .

Diana (*anxious to keep* **Bedales***' attention*) Bread . . . Hugh?

Bedales Oh yes . . . some of my happiest days were spent there. Soft summer afternoons out in the estuary, with a fresh breeze and a trainee receptionist . . . (*He chuckles nostalgically.*)

There is a barely detectable ripple of concern about this last remark, but **Virginia** *sweeps in majestically.*

Virginia Yes, we have some friends in Woodbridge . . . don't we Stephen?

Stephen (*unhelpfully*) Do we have some friends in Woodbridge?

Virginia You know . . . the Mackintoshes.

Bedales Lord and Lady Mackintosh! . . . ?

Virginia No, Mr and Mrs Mackintosh . . .

Bridget (*to* **Bedales**) Oh they're lovely people.

Stephen They might be Lord and Lady, dear . . . have you ever asked them . . . ?

Alan (*to* **Bedales**) What sort of boat was it . . . ?

Bedales Just a Flying Fifteen, standard hull . . .

Stephen I think we should find out. I mean we might have been committing some frightful social gaffe going into their bungalow and addressing them as Ron and Deirdre . . .

Bridget (*losing the irony of course*) No, those must be different Mackintoshes . . . I think *she's* called Prudence . . . Duff and I knew them quite well at one time . . .

Duff Not that well dear . . .

Bridget Weren't you on some sort of committee with him . . . ?

Duff Oh yes. But he's the Chairman. I'm only one of forty-eight co-opted members.

Bridget (*to the table at large*) Terribly, terribly nice people. They used to give a quite splendid garden party every year for about three thousand close friends and it was quite delightful. Bags of salmon, champagne, lots of interesting people and always, without fail, a special table for the estate staff . . . just off to one side . . . which I thought was awfully nice . . . you know.

Stephen (*who has opened another bottle of wine*) What's this committee, Duff?

Virginia (*to* **Bedales**) And what part of the country are you from?

Duff It was a committee of the Rural District . . . Transportation and Access.

Bedales Coldstream . . . the River Tweed . . .

Stephen Anything to do with this container port at Thorpeness?

Duff Yes, that did come up, obviously . . .

Stephen I presume it won't affect us . . .

Duff No . . . no . . . I don't think so . . .

Bedales "Twixt fickle stream and dark o'ercrannied hills' – Scott's country . . .

Stephen Because if it will, obviously we'd have been told about it . . . long in advance mm . . . ?

Duff *looks a little uncomfortable.*

Virginia I used to enjoy Scott a great deal . . .

Diana (*rather sharply*) I don't remember that.

Stephen What did they say on the radio Alan . . . ? About the jolly old container terminal . . .

Virginia (*briskly*) Before you were born dear.

Bedales He was a strange man.

Alan Well as far as I can remember –

Duff (*interjecting*) Stephen that was a terribly inaccurate programme . . .

Bridget Who was strange, Hughsie?

Stephen Oh you heard it then . . . ?

Duff Well of course I *had* to . . . it's part of the job . . .

Bedales 'Woman's faith, and woman's trust – write the characters in dust' . . .

Stephen Whose job is it to tell people who *live* round here what the hell's going on? Or should they just listen to the radio on the off-chance . . .

Bridget He wasn't gay was he . . . ?

Bedales (*with a rich chuckle*) By no means! An appetite as big as his novels.

Virginia (*quickly*) More Shrimp Surprise . . . ?

She reunites the table for a moment. Murmurs of contented rejection.
Stephen *appears not to have heard and buttonholes an increasingly uncomfortable-looking* **Duff**, *once again.*

Stephen Well . . . ? Are we supposed to be mind-readers, Duff . . . ?

Duff Look Stephen, nothing's finalised. There's a lot more talking to be done.

Bedales (*flashing a smile at* **Virginia**) I'd love a little more if I may Mrs Febble . . .

Virginia Oh, for heaven's sake, call me Virginia.

Bedales (*quickly*) Virginia.

Virginia I'll just nip out to the kitchen.

Bedales If it's any trouble . . .

Virginia (*from the kitchen door*) Oh, it's no trouble . . . I'm so glad you like it.

Bedales I love it . . .

Stephen What did you hear on the radio Alan . . . ?

Alan Well I was listening to the programme more from the point of view of the commercial aspects of containerisation in a previously neglected . . .

Stephen (*impatiently*) Yes . . . yes . . . what did you tell me about the road through Canfield . . . ?

Alan They did say there were plans for a six-lane access road through Canfield, which would –

Duff Oh that's absolute nonsense. It'll only be four-lane. At most. And it's not going *through* Canfield, that's the whole point . . . it's going round it . . . that's typical of the programme, which must have been . . .

Stephen So there *is* going to be a container terminal five miles away?

Virginia *appears from the kitchen bearing a glass bowl with fresh Shrimp Surprise in it.*

Virginia It's all done with a bit of ginger and tarragon.

Stephen They'd never get permission . . .

Bedales I've never experienced anything like it before . . .

Virginia (*modestly, as she sits down*) Well, that's the surprise . . .

Bedales One of many, today . . .

Virginia Well, the chicken's going to be fairly ordinary . . . (*She laughs again, nervously.*)

Bedales *smiles.*

Duff They've got permission . . .

Stephen Who the hell from?

Duff Lord Stratforde.

Stephen Stratforde? From Kenham Hall? He's such a sleepy old bugger. You only see him once a year when he opens his gardens on Spring Bank Holiday.

Duff He's not asleep in there Stephen. He's running quite a nice little business you know.

Bedales (*to* **Virginia**, *as she restocks his plate*) Thank you . . . Virginia.

Stephen (*after a pause to digest this*) But surely the council has planning regulations . . .

Duff Oh, of course it does . . . but it also has roads to keep up and hospitals to build and housing to repair and special schools and senior citizens' homes and colleges of Further Education and land reclamation and erosion prevention and drainage and university grants to pay for. So it listens when someone like Stratforde proposes a major international terminal on its crumbling unprofitable coastline . . .

Stephen A major international terminal! Is that what it is now . . . ?

Duff This all *could* be Stephen, nothing is settled . . .

Bedales (*raising his glass*) I don't think anything in the rules prevents a non-drinker from proposing a toast . . . To the cook . . .

Bridget Hear! Hear! Ginny . . .

Duff Oh rather! Superb, Ginny . . .

Stephen *continues, hardly acknowledging the toast.*

Stephen Well just suppose . . . Just suppose there is a major international terminal at Thorpeness, is it not fair to assume that they will have to widen a few country lanes to get to it . . . ?

Diana Daddy, stop talking! Just for once.

Bridget Oh come on you two . . . stop all this business . . .

Duff *doesn't answer. He looks down and slightly shakes his head.* **Virginia** *and* **Diana** *start to clear the table.* **Stephen** *is on another round of wine-pouring.*

Stephen Yes . . . ? Right . . . And given the size of those bloody great lorries that churn up the A12 and scare the hell out of all the drivers over fifty-five in this county . . . they will need to lay at least six country lanes side by side before they can even turn round. Right? So what I hear via Alan, who listened to the radio because he happens to be fascinated by containerisation, poor bugger, is not only likely to be true, but could be a bloody underestimate . . . Mmmm? Am I right? Well, I'm not having my house end up in the middle of a traffic island. And that's what everyone else is going to say round here too . . . isn't it Duff?

Duff *is quiet.*

I mean . . . *isn't it*? You agree don't you . . . You don't want to see our fields and our woods and our cliffs . . . chewed up by bloody juggernauts . . . ? That's not what we've worked all our lives for . . .

Duff There's no point in getting all Churchillian about it, Stephen . . . They're not *our* fields or *our* woods or *our* cliffs . . .

Stephen Well . . . whose are they?

Duff Stratforde's.

Bedales *gets up.*

Bedales May I . . . ? (*He picks up the stacked bowls.*)

Virginia No really . . . you're the . . .

Bedales . . . Uninvited guest. I must do my bit. (*He takes the bowls towards the kitchen.*)

Duff He could put a couple of six-lane highways from the A12 to the coast without having to cut down a single hedge that wasn't his own . . . and still have space left for an airport . . .

Bridget (*picking up two remaining Shrimp Surprise bowls*) Come on, Ginny . . . you can't do all the work tonight . . .

Virginia No, please, Bridget!

Bridget *also goes off to the kitchen motivated, we suspect, more by the desire to observe than serve. As she exits,* **Virginia** *calls to her increasing entourage of helpers.*

Virginia No one's to do a thing.

Alan, *hearing this, leaps up and grabs the brown bread basket.*

Alan I'll bring the bread . . .

Duff I'll bring the Surprise shall I?

He goes and joins the rest in the kitchen.

Stephen *stands silently staring. He drinks.*

Stephen (*slowly, with feeling*) I don't know a bloody thing about anything these days.

The lights slowly fade, leaving a spotlight on **Stephen**. *There is the sharp ring of a telephone.* **Stephen** *looks unblinkingly ahead as we hear the telephone picked up and his voice off:*

Hello, Prime Minister, Febble here . . . I've just come from a meeting about this Canfield motorway business and I felt I ought to tell you that the mood was angry. In fact I'd have to go further and say that, in all honesty, the people round here are hopping mad . . . (*He listens.*) . . . Well, all I can say is that this 'consultation process' has not filtered through to the average man in the village post office and if it had I think the answer would have been a good old Anglo-Saxon 'Up yours!' and a rapid exodus of *Telegraph* readers to the nearest Labour Club . . . Mm? . . . But we *are* the grassroots, Prime Minister, and we may have to be fitted with bleepers in case we fall over but we can still make a cross on a piece of paper when the time comes! . . . What? . . . (*A little flattered.*) . . . no, I'm, not a politician, just a concerned citizen . . . Would I what? . . . Chequers, for the weekend . . . how very nice . . . Will she? . . . No, I don't know her personally. I've seen her on the stamps of course . . . In that case I'm very happy to accept . . . about eight? . . . lovely. Oh, one thing, Prime Minister. Do you and your wife like radishes?

Sound of telephone clicking down. **Stephen** *turns away in the slowly fading spotlight. His shirt is crumpled and has become untucked at the back.*

Fade to blackout. Lights up.

The meal has finished. **Duff** *sits in an armchair.* **Alan** *is on the move towards one of the more uncomfortable upright chairs.* **Bridget** *moves to the sofa with* **Bedales**, *she giggles briefly at something he's said.*

There is a buzz of chat. Everyone seems loosened up. As they make for their places, the table has been cleared, a few wineglasses remain, but **Virginia** *and* **Diana** *are clearing these.*

Virginia *bustles into the kitchen.* **Duff** *calls after her:*

Duff Lovely meal, Ginny . . .

Bedales Excellent . . . The Shrimp Surprise was a delight . . .

Bridget And the Chicken Amazing was fantastic . . .

Bedales And the Pear Supreme was superlative . . .

Gentle, indulgent, after-dinner laughter.

Virginia I'll get some coffee . . .

Everyone sits with well-fed satisfaction.

Stephen . . . ?

Stephen *is at the cocktail cabinet. He looks round quickly.*

Virginia What are you doing?

Stephen Er . . . cigars . . . I was looking for cigars . . .

Virginia (*briskly*) In the sideboard. You specially put them there yesterday . . . remember . . . ?

Bedales I say . . . what's this . . .

He has had trouble leaning back on the sofa and in searching for the obstruction he has revealed **Stephen**'s *hastily hidden blazer. He unfolds it and whistles appreciatively.*

Bedales There's a secret Trinity man amongst us . . . a closet Cantabrian!

Bridget Is this yours Stephen?

Stephen No . . . oh *that* . . . yes . . . yes . . . that's probably one of mine . . . one of my old ones.

Bridget It's not a very good place to keep it . . .

Stephen I don't keep it there . . . I . . . er . . . I put it there to er . . . to . . . make the sofa more comfortable.

Bridget You should wear it . . . it's ever so smart . . .

Stephen *takes the blazer.*

Stephen I don't worry about that sort of thing now . . . Can't go on living in the past . . .

Bedales When were you up?

Stephen (*a touch defiantly*) Fifty-one to fifty-four . . .

Bedales Good Lord . . . we must have been just over the wall from each other . . . I was at Clare . . . I don't remember you . . .

Stephen I don't remember *you*.

Bedales What did you read . . . ?

Stephen History . . .

Bedales Oh . . . you must have known Teddy Lascelles . . . ?

Stephen No . . .

Bedales Horspath . . . ?

Stephen No.

Bedales Victor Robinson . . . Teddy Moncrieff . . .?

Stephen No.

Bedales Marvellous people . . . all wonderfully bright and absolutely irresponsible. Teddy Moncrieff was terribly keen on intercourse. His avowed aim was to get his leg over every girl in Girton. A frightful task. He'd got through twelve when he was run over . . .

Bridget Oh really . . . I don't believe it . . .

Bedales By his best friend . . . Bunty Longstaff. Bunty was pissed as a newt and Teddy was running out of Girton like the clappers having just consummated a relationship with, as rumour has it, the woman who might be our next Archbishop of Canterbury.

Bridget Was he killed? . . .

Bedales Wouldn't have been . . . but Bunty backed the car up to see if he could help, went straight over him *again*!

Bridget Oh no . . .

Bedales Bunty was the one I felt sorry for. He never recovered from running over one of the greatest minds of his generation. Went quite potty, joined the Rhodesian Police and thrashed someone to death.

Bridget You men were so lucky. I was stuck in a simply frightful establishment in the North . . . There were a hundred and forty girls there and sixteen dogs . . .

Alan *Dogs?*

Bridget Guard dogs . . . It was a sort of top-security girls' school. Emphasis on manly virtues. You know . . . heaps of exercise, walking, running, climbing the fells. The result was that after five years they produced enormously strong women with insatiable sexual appetites . . . Well of course the inevitable happened . . .

Bedales What?

Bridget Gang rape.

Stephen Gang rape . . . ! . . . ?

Bridget Fourteen sixth formers attacked the visiting chaplain. He was quite a young man – he'd come to give a talk on missionary work in Central Africa.

Duff What happened . . . ?

Bridget We were all gated, of course.

Duff No, what happened to *him*?

Bridget He had a crisis of conscience. Ended up at the BBC.

Virginia *enters, bearing coffee tray with cups, jug and milk thereon.*

Virginia (*setting it down*) Now then . . . coffees? . . . Bridget.

Bridget Oh, yes please Ginny dear . . .

Virginia Hugh . . . ?

Bedales Oh please . . .

Duff We shouldn't be too late dear . . .

Bridget Oh come on . . . Duff . . . I'm just beginning to enjoy myself . . . (*to* **Virginia**) We were talking about our murky pasts, darling . . .

Duff I was only thinking of our hosts . . . they've had a busy day . . .

Stephen How about our murky presents eh?

He proffers a cigar. He's obviously on the way to becoming very drunk. He's talking too loudly for one thing.

Duff No thanks old chap . . .

Stephen That's what interests me . . .

He throws the cigars down without offering them to anyone else, and takes one out himself. **Virginia** *looks up.*

Virginia Stephen . . . aren't you going to offer one to Hugh . . . ?

Bedales Very kind, but I'm not a great cigar man. I think I shall stick to one of my 'herbal' cigarettes if you don't mind . . .

Bedales *pulls out a silver cigarette case from which he withdraws a carefully prepared joint. Not that* **Stephen** *notices.*

Stephen Oh . . . a *herbal* cigarette . . . of course . . .

Bedales *lights up and inhales deeply.* **Stephen** *goes on goadingly.*

Stephen . . . Would you care for a little Eau de Maison with your 'herbal' cigarette. Perhaps some Château Hot-Tap this time . . . mmm?

Virginia Darling you can be very unfunny.

Stephen I try my best dear . . . (*He turns to Hugh.*) My God . . . it smells like manure . . .

He laughs but no one else does.

Virginia (*innocently*) What are they actually Hugh . . . ?

Bedales A very mild form of cannabis.

Stephen's *laughter freezes.*

Stephen What? . . . !

Bedales Extremely mild.

There is quite a stir at this. **Virginia** *looks a little askance and after a brief pause* **Stephen** *becomes quite animated.*

Stephen Put it out!

Diana (*with a short laugh*) Oh . . . *Daddy* . . . !

Stephen We'll get arrested . . .

Bedales I very much doubt it . . .

Stephen (*very agitated*) That stuff is illegal!

Virginia (*confused*) It isn't is it?

Stephen It bloody well is . . . !

Bedales (*reassuringly*) Oh yes, it is illegal . . .

Stephen That's what I mean! And I'm the householder . . . I'm the one who goes to prison! Well I'm not doing ten years for someone who wasn't even invited! . . . So you'd better put the bloody thing out and smoke a cigar like any other normal human being.

Bedales (*quite unruffled*) It's quite all right, Mr Febble . . . I *am* on the medical register . . . I take it on prescription . . .

Stephen On prescription eh! Are you telling me *our* Health Service prescribes *drugs*!

Bedales *chuckles genially at this.* **Alan** *and* **Diana** *also snigger* . . . **Stephen** *looks hurt and flushes briefly at his solecism.*

Bridget Why don't we all have one?

Virginia Bridget . . . !

Bridget It's ever so nice . . .

Duff You've never had it, darling . . .

Bridget (*quickly*) No . . . no . . . but . . . er . . . I've heard about it.

Stephen (*he's looking dangerous now. He turns drunkenly towards them*) Very clever . . . very funny . . . My ignorance is really appalling is it not . . .

Alan There are many different types of cannabis aren't there . . . ? I heard a programme on Radio 3 a couple of years ago . . .

Stephen I mean *I* didn't know that Duff was lying to me about his little plans for self-advancement on the local council eh . . . ?

Virginia Stephen! Liqueurs I think . . .

Stephen Do you know, Bridget . . . I didn't even know you were coming to dinner tonight . . . It's all a wonderful surprise . . .

Virginia Stephen!

But he's enjoying his performance.

Stephen Oh, there's no *limit* to the amount I don't know . . . I mean for all I know Bridget could be having an affair with the vicar . . . or even our friend the foot surgeon here . . . and *I'd* never know a damn thing about it. Ha! Ha! Ha! Ha . . .

Bridget And if you didn't know it, you'd invent it I suppose . . . (*She laughs.*)

Stephen Yes . . . that's right Bridget . . . I'd rack my little brains and try and invent something to make your life sound a little more interesting? Add a little sparkle . . . eh?

Virginia Stephen! *Offer* the liqueurs!

Stephen Getting a little near the knuckle . . . eh, darling?

Virginia (*losing her patience*) A brandy, Duff?

She gets up and crosses to the drinks table, taking a brandy glass off the shelf as she does so.

Stephen I'll do it . . . I'll do it.

He moves unsteadily toward the drinks and removes the glass stopper from the decanter, but pauses then, holding it.

. . . I mean look at us all sitting round here tonight . . . (*He pours a brandy.*)

What a shame it is that we're all so normal . . . so predictable, so well brought up . . . so bereft of any interesting little secrets . . . (*He drinks the brandy.*)

Virginia Stephen! That's Duff's brandy!

Duff (*to* **Virginia**) Help myself . . . shall I . . . ?

Virginia I think you'd better . . .

Stephen Yes . . . help yourself to anyone Duff . . . anyone in this room . . . *I'll* tell *you* a secret . . . Virginia's very fond of you you know . . . She's always had a soft spot for you . . . especially when you wear your little shorts in the summer.

As **Stephen** *moves in on* **Duff**, *others smile politely and a little desperately.*

Stephen . . . I think she'd probably quite like to have those little shorts off you, Duff . . . creep up behind you one day when you're mowing the lawn . . . late August when the aquilegia's fading and those lean and wiry desert legs of yours are straining away at the Qualcast . . . I don't think she'd even wait for you to empty the grass box . . . There and then, over and over in the japonica as the Qualcast spins out of control towards the kitchen extension.

Stephen *laughs ironically to himself, then pauses, staring down ruminatively.*

A long and gloomy pause. He closes on **Duff** *confidingly.*

. . . Don't think I couldn't exist without Virginia . . . What do I really need her for – I'm not incontinent, I'm not immobile, I can get from the sofa to the television in 4.6 seconds . . . I can cook. Curries. Superb curries. She never lets me do them. I wouldn't mind being alone you know. Curry, television and the *Telegraph*. Not a bad life. No pretence Duff . . . no having to smile and grin and behave and gossip and keep up the old show of respectability until you respectably drop dead. When I die, which'll probably be bloody soon if the TV programmes don't get any better, I shall give my heart, lungs, liver and any other offaly bits to the nation and then I shall have the rest burnt and my ashes scattered over the entrance to the Channel Tunnel as a welcoming gesture to foreigners.

He laughs shortly, mirthlessly.

Bridget Duff, it's time to go . . .

Stephen . . . I'm glad we had this little chat Duff . . . It's been worrying me in a silly way . . . I didn't sleep a wink last night . . .

Bridget Come on, you two.

Stephen I know, Duff's brandy . . . I haven't forgotten. (*He turns to the drinks table.*)

Virginia They are going.

Stephen Going already?

Duff It's after eleven.

Bridget We mustn't be too late . . . Lots of packing to do, and I hate doing it last thing.

Virginia I quite agree. Get as much done tonight as you can . . .

Duff God knows what I'll be putting in . . . the state I'm in . . .

Laughter, except from **Stephen**.

Stephen Packing? Where are you going . . .

Virginia Honestly, Stephen, you don't listen to a thing!

Duff We're off to sunny Italy for a week . . .

Stephen Who?

Duff The two of us . . .

Stephen You and Gin – ?

Duff Bridget, yes . . .

Bridget Absolute surprise! Suddenly came out with it at breakfast last Thursday.

Duff Got a letter from a friend out there. We were in the Paras together. They took him to Italy full of shrapnel and he stayed there. Started a garage – mostly out of army surplus I gather . . . Anyway, we'll do a recce for you and maybe you two could go out there later. I don't think he'd charge.

Virginia Italy isn't really Stephen's sort of thing . . .

Stephen (*grimly*) No. Too much culture.

A few laughs, but not from **Stephen**.

Duff Well, thanks for a very . . . jolly evening . . . sorry we're the killjoys . . . Bye-bye Ginny, my love . . .

He kisses her briefly.

Virginia Bye-bye Duff . . . have a lovely holiday.

Duff Bye-bye Stephen . . .

Bridget *turns to* **Stephen**.

Bridget Bye-bye, Stephen.

She kisses him, slightly more fully.

Voices fade as **Virginia**, **Duff** *and* **Bridget** *exit into the hall, followed by* **Diana** *and* **Alan**, *everyone being bravely cheerful.*

Bedales (*holding out his hand*) Farewell Mr Febble. It was lovely to see your home. I hope you will feel free to make full use of mine when you are in London. I gather I may be seeing you in a couple of weeks . . .

Stephen Me . . . ? Why . . .

Bedales Well, as Virginia is going to be there anyway, she rather sensibly suggested that the two of you come. Make a weekend of it. I gather you don't travel as much as you used to . . .

Stephen Virginia, in London, what the hell for?

Bedales It's her first appointment. (*He shakes hands firmly.*)

Bedales *crosses the room and turns.*

She has problems too you know! (*He goes.*)

Stephen *stands without speaking. After a moment* **Diana** *comes back in.*

Stephen The smarmy, dirty . . . cheap little bastard!

Diana He's not cheap, Daddy . . . that's for sure.

Diana *starts clearing up. Like her mother it's a sort of instinctive reaction. The tenser the atmosphere the more intense the clearing. At the moment she's putting a few ashtrays and coffee-cups onto the table.*

Stephen There's nothing wrong with her feet.

Diana (*picking up her half-finished coffee and coming round to sit on the sofa*) Everybody's got something wrong with their feet.

Stephen *turns to her, about to say something. But he swallows air for a moment, shuts his mouth and starts again.*

Stephen What?

Diana That's what he said. He's quite a clever man.

Stephen Clever! Him . . . ! That devious little dope-peddler . . . ?

Diana It didn't seem to affect him at all.

Stephen You saw him. Cannabis in his cigarette. Right in front of the window.

Diana Daddy, Canfield hasn't got a policeman, let alone a Drug Squad!

Stephen *goes across to the cabinet and reaches for the scotch.*

Stephen . . . He's a quack, a charlatan . . . he's never done a decent day's work in his life. Scuffling around at people's feet in a cloud of heroin all afternoon . . . You know what *he's* after. Well, I wouldn't let him near mine, I tell you that. I wouldn't let him below my waist for a second . . . (*Mimics him.*) . . . 'She sensibly suggested the two of you might like to come.'

Virginia (*entering*) Having some more dear?

Stephen (*holding a scotch bottle, unscrewed and about to pour*) No . . . no . . . just rearranging the bottles in time for Christmas . . . I thought it was about time the Cherry Heering was at the front again . . .

He tips a large and undisciplined slug of scotch into his glass, and swings round before she can say anything.

. . . What is this, Virginia? What the hell are you doing with that fucking little phoney?

Diana I'm going to bed.

Stephen (*snapping*) You stay!

Diana No!

Virginia *has stopped her incipient attempt at clearing up. She looks suddenly older, wearier, defenceless for the first time.*

Virginia (*to* **Diana**) Goodnight, darling . . . lie-in tomorrow . . . ?

Diana (*without much enthusiasm*) . . . Yes, please.

Virginia I won't wake you.

Diana *comes across and kisses* **Virginia** *briefly. She goes.* **Virginia** *looks across to* **Stephen**.

Virginia (*gently*) Why don't you go to bed as well? It's quite late . . . and you're tired . . . We can talk about everything in –

Stephen Listen . . . I know you can't stand me. I know you find me a lout and a boor and a drunkard, but why the fucking hell do you go crawling to that overpaid slippery little fornicator who leaves a stink like a pop singer in *my* living room. How can you possibly entertain the thought of being . . . manipulated by that . . . rodent . . . let alone *paying* for the privilege!

Virginia (*with effort*) I am not paying, if you must know he's seeing me for nothing . . .

Stephen Oh is he! *Is* he! *Is* he now?

Virginia Go to bed . . .

She starts to clear up, very briskly.

Stephen No thank you, I'm fine. Never felt wider awake . . . I shall sit here, in *my* sitting room, and consume *my* whisky at a leisurely pace and talk to *my* wife as people do all over the country – STOP CLEARING UP!

The force of his final shout freezes **Virginia**.

Leave things *alone*! This is a home not an intensive care unit . . . ! (*Quietening.*) Ginny . . . (*He motions to the sofa.*) sit down . . . have a drink (*He goes round to the drinks cabinet.*) . . . for once just have a drink . . . with me . . .

Virginia (*sitting, her face set impassively, back held very straight*) Bitter lemon . . .

Stephen Bitter lemon . . . ?

He sighs with a shrug of desperation.

(*Pleading.*) Have something *with* the bitter lemon . . . for God's sake . . . a little Dubonnet . . . ? A sliver of gin (*He ruffles around with the bottles in the cabinet.*) . . . Cherry Heering? Very cheering . . . Cherry Heering . . .

Virginia Bitter lemon and ice.

Stephen Ice! Ice . . . now you're talking . . . Nothing like a nice little lump of ice to relax you. (*Opens ice bucket.*) There you go. (*He extracts the tongs.*) . . . How many bergs . . . of ice?

Virginia *says nothing.*

. . . well, let's start with two . . . (*He pops them in.*) . . . Don't want to hurtle out of control straight away . . .

He hands the glass to **Virginia**, *who still sits impassively – nobly, almost on the edge of the sofa. She accepts the glass without acknowledgement.* **Stephen** *turns back towards the drinks table.*

Stephen And for me? . . . mm . . . I think I'll stick to Doctor Dewar's Patent Medicine . . . for the forlorn in heart . . . Hmmm . . .

Chuckles as he pours himself another liberal glass of scotch, screws the top back on in a studied and leisurely way, and comes back to the armchair opposite **Virginia**.

Stephen . . . Now . . . we can talk . . .

He sits heavily. Looks across at **Virginia**, *and raises his glass.*

. . . Now we can talk . . .

There is a pause. **Virginia** *does not move her glass to her lips. It remains in her hand. Her body is still perfectly straight. It is unnerving for a moment until we realise that she is crying.*

Almost imperceptibly and without any hanging of the head. Nobly, in fact. Slowly but surely the sobbing increases. It comes from very deep and throughout she maintains a composure. A battle between intensely felt emotion and years of breeding, which have conditioned her not to show it. She sets down her glass, and leaves.

Slowly the light fades and narrows into a spot on **Stephen**.

Then a light goes on, and the front door slams.

The lights come up again. **Alan** *stands at the light switch.*

Alan Oh, hello Grandpa.

He turns, brushes some dog hairs off his coat. He looks around.

Everyone gone . . . have they?

Stephen No . . . no. . . they're all hiding.

Alan *Hiding?*

Stephen *doesn't bother to reply. He shakes his head then looks down into his empty glass.* **Alan** *stands a little awkwardly and uneasily.*

Alan . . . I'm sorry Grandad . . . was I interrupting . . . something?

Stephen No . . . no . . . we were just . . . er . . . Bitter lemon's such a pissy awful drink don't you think . . .

Alan Well it's all right, quite refreshing . . .

Stephen No, it's not all right . . . it's a miserable mean tight-arsed little drink . . . I mean if you're the sort of joyless sod who can't cope with alcoholic beverages then why the hell not try ginger beer or even tonic . . . something with a bit of style . . . but for Christ's sake deliver us from bitter lemon . . . spinstery little poison . . . it *reeks* of disapproval . . .

Alan (*a little embarrassed maybe*) Yes . . . well I've got Pippa down . . . Had rather a bright idea . . . popped her in the back of the Volvo, dropped down the back seat. Seventy-five cubic feet to roam around in.

Stephen Have a drink . . . (*He heaves himself to his feet and makes for the drinks table.*)

Alan (*doubtfully*) Well . . . I think it's bed for –

Stephen (*sharply*) Oh come on! What the hell's wrong with everybody . . . All I asked was if you wanted a bloody drink. It's not the greatest moral decision of your life for Christ's sake . . . !

Alan Well, all right . . . er . . . I'll have a bitter lemon . . .

Stephen (*astounded*) You . . . what . . .

But he's been wrong-footed. **Alan** *is grinning sheepishly and looking a little pleased with himself . . .*

Stephen Ahh (*He grunts with pleasure and surprise.*) . . . very good
. . . very good . . . Brandy?

Alan Thank you.

Stephen *picks up the decanter and starts to pour. He chuckles again to
himself and shakes his head. He picks up the glass and brings it across to*
Alan.

Stephen You know – forgive me for saying this – but I used to
think you were a boring little fart . . .

Alan I used to think you were a pompous old prick . . .

Stephen *tenses for a split second, then convulses with approving laughter,
as* **Alan** *watches modestly.*

Stephen I like that . . . I *like* that (*More laughter.*) . . . oh yes . . .

He finally brings his laughter under control. He pours himself another.

Why is it the youth of today has so little respect for pompous old
pricks . . . mm . . . ? You know . . . I'm getting younger. I
reckon I'm about eighteen now. Obstinate, opinionated,
unreceptive, suspicious, self-pitying, obsessive and frightened of
the future.

Alan Why do you always pretend you don't like anybody?

Stephen (*indignantly*) I do not pretend . . . ! Listen, Alan
Containerisation . . . when you reach the age of eighteen again
. . . when *you* go through the agonies of a second adolescence . . .
you will realise that there is precious little in this shitty world *to*
like.

Stephen *sits heavily, ungracefully, back into his chair, spilling a little of
his ample scotch onto his tie. He mops it perfunctorily.*

Alan You've not done so badly . . .

Stephen (*a mocking mirthless laugh*) Ha . . . ! I've done *everything*
badly . . . that's the message that comes through to me loud and
clear every single waking moment. It's a hell of a thing to realise
at my age . . . It's a hell of a thing to realise that life is nearly
done and you have cocked it up . . .

Alan That's the whisky talking . . .

Stephen (*sharply, very vehemently*) Shut up! I'll drink if I want . . .

Very deliberately, with eyes blazing defiance, he swigs back the rest of his substantial glass of scotch. He winces briefly as if at some hidden pain, then with an enormous and deliberate effort he gets to his feet and walks around the head of the sofa to the drinks table. With a hard and defiant stare at **Alan** *he refills his glass, raises it to his lips and with a quick and triumphant flick of the wrist downs it in its entirety. He holds the empty glass in front of him, with a challenging smile of achievement. Then he fills the glass, and walks, again with superbly controlled effort, back to the chair, and sits without a moment's loss of balance. Only then does he lean back and appraise* **Alan**.

Stephen As I was saying before I was so rudely interrupted, this weekend has reminded me rather sharply of this fact . . .

Alan I'm sorry . . . ?

Stephen Do pay attention . . . I was talking, was I not, of the realisation that one has got one's life wrong. I'm not a Hindu, I don't expect to come back as a cow . . . I'm not a Catholic so I cannot enjoy the solace of knowing that the more I cock it up the more God loves me . . . and I'm not at all sure that there is any hereafter at all . . . of any kind . . . anywhere . . . So this has been my shot, and I will not be given another . . . and I had better get used to the fact that I have made a pig's arse of it . . .

Alan You've got Virginia and your friends, and Diana . . .

Stephen Just a moment! Not so fast! . . . Let's take that point by point. 'I have Virginia. Discuss.' . . . Well, I have a woman in this house who tries to get on with her life despite my lingering presence. I have a woman in this house who irons my underpants and turns the television off when I fall asleep in front of it. I don't have Virginia. *Others* have Virginia. Point two. 'I have a friend.' . . . I *had*, as I thought, a friend . . . a man whom even I could talk to . . . whom I respected and almost admired. Since this . . . horrendous weekend began . . . I know him to be a pitiful cuckolded liar . . . a man who would share as much with me as he wanted . . . and no more . . . He's not a friend . . . any more than Virginia's a wife. Diana . . . well, she's yours now, not mine . . . and she can do just what she wants . . . for all I care . . . and I hear she's about to do just that . . .

Alan She told you that . . . ?

Stephen No! She didn't tell me anything . . . (*A touch savagely.*)
No one told me *anything*. I think I probably read it in the
Telegraph. After Births and Deaths. 'Marriages on the Rocks.'
The relationship between Diana Mary Wallis and Alan Wallis is
slowly going down the plughole at their lovely home in Wath-on-
Dearne. No . . . No one told me. Is she bored with you . . . ? She
always was . . . a bit volatile . . . What's the problem Alan . . .
feeling unloved . . . ?

Alan Well . . . no . . . it's rather the opposite . . . I er . . . (*He
drains his brandy.*) I'm afraid I've met somebody else . . .

Stephen (*momentarily stunned*) *You've* met somebody else . . . ?

Alan Someone I work with . . .

Stephen (*incredulously*) You mean you've found someone *else*
who's attracted to *you*?

Alan (*as usual, unaware of any irony*) I think she is, yes . . .

Stephen You *think* she is. Don't you think you'd better find out
first . . . ? It sounds extremely unlikely to me.

Alan I think this is the real thing . . .

Stephen Real infidelity.

Alan *goes on doggedly.*

Alan Since Diana and I were married I've had a few
relationships with other women but they never came to anything.
Then I met Christine and –

Stephen A *few*?

Alan You know, just one night . . . flings . . .

Stephen (*with genuine incredulity*) How many . . . ?

Alan In the job . . . you know . . .

Stephen How *many*?

Alan (*reluctantly*) Well . . .

Stephen Two . . . ? Three . . . ? Eighty-seven . . . ?

Alan (*uncomfortably*) Well . . . nearer eighty-seven . . .

Stephen How *dare* you tell me this . . .

Alan . . . They were just purely physical . . .

Stephen How . . . ? Where from . . . ?

Alan Well . . . you know what my job involves . . . containerisation development and –

Stephen Yes . . . yes . . . yes . . . Don't for God's sake go into all that . . .

Alan Well over the last ten years as you know there's been something of a revolution in bulk cargo handling techniques . . .

Stephen (*impatiently*) Yes . . .

Alan This involves a certain amount of work with the local planning offices. Investigating building investment controls, land development restrictions, environmental guidelines and this is where the problem begins . . .

Stephen *nods uncomprehendingly.*

Alan Planning offices . . .

Stephen *is lost.*

Alan Spending two or three nights every week in Middlesbrough or King's Lynn or Lowestoft isn't easy . . .

Stephen I can believe that . . .

Alan I think Diana knew . . . something was up.

Stephen (*still in stunned astonishment*) Something was *up*?

Alan . . . But she never questioned me and it honestly never altered my feelings for her or the children at all – honestly. But Chris is rather different . . .

Stephen Planning Office . . . ?

Alan (*nods*) Chatham. A forty-eight-acre site qualifying for a regional support grant. Six-berth roll-on roll-off facilities. When the final contracts were being worked out, I was spending two or three weeks at a stretch down there . . .

There is a pause. **Alan** *spreads his arms and shrugs.*

It happens. I mean that's the sort of thing everybody does every now and then . . . It's a fact of life isn't it . . . ?

Stephen It wasn't one of the facts of life I was taught.

Alan But in all *your* married life you must have been . . .

Stephen (*unhelpfully*) Yes . . . ?

Alan Er . . . in the same situation yourself.

Stephen No.

Alan Not once . . . ?

Stephen No.

Alan In thirty-nine years?

Stephen I would remember.

Alan Well, I think at some time, everyone wants someone else . . . Just physically you know . . .

Stephen Diana and Virginia as well I suppose.

Alan Well, no, I'm talking about men.

Stephen (*a little ironic smile*) Ah . . .

Alan I mean, men's needs are different . . . you know . . . physically . . .

Stephen I wish you'd stop using that word. Life isn't a bloody PT display.

Alan Well, you know what I mean. (*He gets up and goes to replenish his brandy.*)

Stephen Didn't you ever talk to her about it?

Alan Well of course we talked. But it's never easy with the kids around – and the dog to take for a walk . . .

Stephen Takes quite a lot of looking after . . . the dog, eh?

Alan Pippa? Yes, I should say so . . .

Stephen You know where you went wrong? You should have married the dog and had Diana as a pet . . .

Alan Very funny . . .

Stephen You'd have made a very good dog, Alan . . . I can see you in your element now, sniffing around telegraph poles; peeing on car wheels, rubbing your arse up against the wall, having a quick scratch before trotting after the next backside. You don't deserve anybody you scum.

Alan Look, you asked me and I was truthful with you . . .

Stephen Get out!

Stephen *is standing. Eyes ablaze.* **Alan** *moves back.*

Alan Diana was absolutely right about you . . . it's always you . . . the world is always you . . . never anybody else . . .

Stephen Of all the scum I've seen today, you are the worst . . . the most degrading . . . You make me feel like a saint . . . you bastard!

Stephen *swings wildly, and falls gracelessly as the sofa overturns beneath his weight. He disappears.* **Alan** *looks down at him then exits.*

Stephen *lies like a beached whale unable to move. With a great effort he pulls himself up to a kneeling position. Gradually he raises his head. He looks towards the window, then down at his watch. He stares at it for a long time.*

Stephen (*to himself*) Alaric's my friend. *He* knows how to deal with me. Stays out eighteen hours a day . . .

He stands and walks, tucking his crumpled clothes in, slowly round past the dinner table to the french window. He looks suddenly crumpled, bowed and old.

Stephen *lifts his tumbler to his lips and drains the glass. Then he opens the door . . . and calls out, thickly.*

Stephen Alaric . . . al . . . ar . . . ic . . . !

He pauses for a moment, then hurls one final frenzied bellow at the darkness outside. A bellow full of desperation and a howl of pain.

ALARICCCCCCC!!

Fade to blackout.

Sunday.

The **Febbles**' *living room. Early morning. There is not much natural light yet and we cannot make out the details of the room very clearly.*

After a moment or two to establish this pre-dawn light, a shape appears suddenly at the sitting-room door. It's **Virginia**. *She completes the tying of a belt around a white, almost luminous dressing-gown.*

Virginia Stephen . . . ?

No sound.

Stephen . . . ?

There is, after a short pause, an answering grunt from the sofa. **Stephen** *lies, hand tucked under his head, the length of the sofa. He is still in his clothes.*

Virginia What *are* you doing?

Stephen Thinking.

Virginia Do you know what the time is . . . ?

Stephen (*after a moment's deliberation*) Nineteen hundred and . . . something or other.

Virginia It's half-past four.

Another pause.

Stephen I'm waiting for the dawn.

Virginia You must be frozen. The heating doesn't come on till six . . .

Stephen No, I'm warm . . .

Virginia Come to bed. You'll be in a terrible state in the morning.

She reaches down, without thinking, and picks up **Alan**'s *glass, which she transfers tidily to a tray on the sideboard.*

Stephen It *is* the morning.

Virginia *turns from the sideboard and looks down at her husband. With some emotion around the pity area. Then she moves to the door and switches* *on the lights. Not many, perhaps a few lamps, so we can detect the early signs of dawn as the scene progresses.*

Virginia (*having seemed about to say something else*) Do you want a cup of tea?

Stephen (*brightening, and looking up as if returning from a different place of contemplation to the real world*) Bravo!

Virginia *goes out to the kitchen. We hear her preparing the tea – running water into kettle, getting cups out of cupboard and arranging them on tray etc.*

Stephen *rises from the sofa. He coughs and after a moment's unsteadiness, walks slowly to the french windows and stands for a moment looking out. He pushes them open, yawns, breathes deeply, but coughs involuntarily at the force of the fresh air. He has to gasp for breath. He reaches back for a chair, almost falling as he goes. He sits, bent double. There is no sound from him for a moment until breath returns again in short sharp gasps. A kettle boils and by the time* **Virginia** *returns he's recovered. She sets a tea tray down on the dinner table.*

Stephen I sorted Alan out.

Virginia Oh . . .

Stephen Well what's the use of a family if you can't talk.

Virginia That's good, coming from you.

Stephen What d'you mean?

Virginia Oh . . . Stephen (*She laughs incredulously.*) . . . the way you behave when you *do* have a family to talk to.

Stephen Oh . . . that's just a game . . .

Virginia Well, it's a silly game dear . . . why do you play it?

Stephen (*recovered now, and anxious not to show any trace of pain to* **Virginia**) Well I can't stand all this soppy smooching 'how wonderful to see you dear' . . . kiss kiss peck peck sort of nonsense that you're so good at.

Virginia You're just frightened of showing affection.

Stephen That's not affection . . . it's ritual. It's always the same . . . 'Hello *darling*' . . . 'How *lovely* to see you . . . how was the *journey?'* You'd say exactly the same if she was standing there holding an axe dripping with blood. 'Hello darling . . . how are you . . . how was the *journey?'*

Virginia Doesn't it ever occur to you Stephen that I may be *really desperately* pleased to see them?

Stephen I know . . . I know . . .

Virginia No, you *don't* know! Even greater than my pleasure at seeing them is the fear that one day, one day . . . you will drive them away and they'll never come back.

Stephen I love to see them too.

Virginia Well, why don't you ever show it . . . ?

There is a pause. **Stephen** *spoons two sugars into his cup and stirs, then sets down the spoon. He speaks deliberately.*

Stephen I'm not *good* at showing that I like people . . . It frightens me.

Virginia What are you frightened *of* . . . ?

Stephen Of . . . Of people having to like me back . . .

Virginia (*she gives a despairing half-laugh*) Oh . . . !

Stephen Because I never believe it when they do. I know that they're just being nice . . . it's not affection, it's condescension . . .

Virginia *joins him at the table. She pours herself a cup of tea.*

Virginia I didn't know you had such a poor opinion of yourself . . .

Stephen All part of my defensive system . . .

Virginia And so you go straight into the attack . . .

Stephen Sort of . . .

Virginia The pre-emptive strike . . . ?

Stephen Where did you learn that?

Virginia From watching you – over a hundred weekends!

Stephen Oh hell . . . ! I don't . . . I don't mean . . . I don't *mean* to . . .

Virginia (*softly*) Drink your tea . . . it's getting cold . . .

Absently he spoons in another spoonful of sugar and stirs, but doesn't drink. A trace of a smile, a reflection of a happy memory crosses his face.

Stephen I remember the first time Diana left home. She was six or seven. We were living in Driffield.

Virginia I don't remember that . . .

Stephen No, you were out shopping, I think. I believe I'd committed some offence against her tortoise – moved it from one side of the lawn to the other . . . to avoid it blunting the blades of the lawnmower. But Di didn't see it like that at all and I think we had a sort of healthy yell at each other and the next thing she'd packed a carrier bag with all her worldly possessions and buggered off. She said she was going to go all the way to America, but the bag broke just outside the post office – two apples, a blanket, some string, four pieces of coal and one of my old maps of Worcestershire.

Virginia Were there great tears . . . ?

Stephen Oh floods . . . hydroelectric scheme . . . right there on the pavement. Mondisham was out of her front door like greased lightning . . .

Virginia Miss Mondisham! I haven't thought about her for years. (*She takes a sip of tea.*) She buttonholed me once in the butcher's . . . about your khaki shorts.

Stephen My khaki shorts . . . ?

Virginia She claimed she could see one of your testicles when you were weeding the rockery . . .

Stephen *laughs heartily at this.*

Virginia Only visible during the winter, she said . . . when the leaves had fallen off that beech hedge . . .

Stephen *laughs long and loud, and* **Virginia** *too, after which there is a silence.*

Stephen (*eventually, sadly*) They don't make underpants like that any more –

Virginia (*slowly, rather matter of factly*) I loved you when we lived in Driffield.

Stephen *looks up at her.*

I mean, the house wasn't much, and you hated working at Cox's, but . . . there was something exciting about it all . . .

Stephen We haven't used that word for years . . .

Virginia (*more briskly, less reflectively*) No . . . well, we've been busy . . .

She picks up the teapot. She's about to pour, when she looks closely at him for the first time. She pauses, then speaks with genuine concern.

Stephen, you look exhausted . . . I mean . . . *really* exhausted . . . Please come to bed.

Stephen (*with sudden urgency*) No, no . . . Pour the tea . . . We're talking to each other. It doesn't happen that often . . .

Virginia Stephen . . . look what the time is . . .

Stephen What the hell does it matter what the time is! What is the appointed time for two human beings to talk to each other? Tea-time? After eleven but before three . . . ?

Virginia (*getting up and making for the door*) Don't shout . . . I can't take any more shouting . . .

Stephen (*following her*) This is the off-peak period, it's cheaper to talk now! Please . . . ?

Virginia *pauses, her back to him.*

Stephen I'm sorry . . . that I drank too much last night and shouted . . . But that's the way I am Ginny . . . I drink . . . I hate dogs and dinner parties. I make wrong decisions, I shout and I have no friends any more. I can't change now, Ginny . . . it's too late.

She turns towards him.

Virginia Stephen . . . when we lived in Driffield you used to drink – you hated dogs, you were argumentative and you didn't

like dinner parties, but we got on so well . . . You were very
funny . . .

Stephen Aren't I still funny?

Virginia In those days you made jokes that made us *all* laugh –
not just yourself. You were always doing things wrong – but at
least you were doing things, not waiting behind your newspaper
for someone else to make the move and then shooting them down
for making it.

There is a pause. **Virginia** *looks towards the window.* **Stephen** *pours
some more tea and takes a cup over to* **Virginia** *as she sits on the sofa.*

Virginia You gave up a little didn't you . . . ?

Stephen Didn't you . . . ? Moving every six months . . . ?

Virginia No, I didn't mind. I was proud of you for not just
taking anything . . .

Stephen (*with an ironic groan*) Oh Ginny . . .

Virginia No, I mean it. There's no loss of face in turning things
down. If it's not what you want . . . if you're not being used
properly . . . I think that's quite courageous – lots of people in
those days would have just sat there and accepted any job. I
loved you for that.

Stephen Ginny . . . Ginny . . . (*He speaks slowly.*) I wasn't
turning anything down.

Virginia That's what you told me.

Stephen Because I couldn't come home in the evening and tell
you that the Head of Sales had had me in his office and told me
I was a liability to the company . . . I couldn't come home and
bounce Diana up and down on my knee and tell her I'd heard
myself described as a 'professional drunk' by giggling office boys
in the toilet!

Virginia You were a Sales Manager.

Stephen One of seventeen working for an Area Manager who
was responsible to a Local Manager who was responsible to a
National Manager who was responsible to a Sales Director who

was responsible to the Board who probably all came from
Trinity College, Cambridge and who despised me.

Virginia Don't be ridiculous.

Stephen You liked Bristol so much I never had the courage to
tell you.

Virginia Tell me what?

Stephen One day I found a note in my pay packet, 'In view of
organisational rationalisation your position has been regraded'
£500 a year less. Just a note that was all. Well I went to see him
– the Area Manager – I was old enough to be his father. I
remember it was November 5th and I was worried about missing
Di's party. I asked him what it was all about. He said he wanted
to be straight and blunt . . . but did I realise that two major
customers had gone elsewhere since I took over. Had I heard
that there had been four separate complaints from people in my
department about my abusive behaviour. (*He smiles briefly at this.*)
He said as far as he was concerned I was lucky to get away with
a pay cut. The only reason I hadn't been sacked was because the
Personnel Director had also been to Cambridge. He sat behind
his desk and he looked at me with utter contempt. That was the
lowest point I ever reached.

Virginia You never –

Stephen No let me tell you. I left the Old Bell after an hour of
swift scotches, and I walked, somehow, up to Clifton, and out
along the suspension bridge. And I reached the middle and at
that moment in time nothing in the world seemed more pleasant
than to hurtle at 130 feet per second into the dark and all-
embracing waters below. A wonderful deliverance – heady
freedom, rushing wind, crack, and oblivion. Nothing more
expected. No more explanations, no more lies or failures . . . But
it's not as easy to throw yourself off a bridge as it sounds.
Specially when you've had nineteen scotches. You've got to
heave yourself up onto the parapet with the balance of a bloody
gymnast. Well I couldn't manage it at all . . . I just didn't have
the skill . . . so I leaned over the side and threw up . . . and the
wind caught the contents and blew them away to the north-west
. . . onto the bonnets of the cars streaming homewards, way
below me. The knowledge that one of those cars might have

contained the Area Manager cheered me a little, and I washed in the fountain at Queen's Road and got home in time to let off a few rockets for Diana and go 'Ooh . . . Aah' at the Emerald Rain. You know . . . I sometimes wish that I hadn't been so pissed.

Virginia Stephen!

Stephen No. On balance I'm very glad I *was* too pissed. I was safe from then on . . . and I've been safe ever since . . . safe but neutralised . . . allowed to survive but only on the lowest and least troublesome level of existence. And that's why I drink and shout and abuse you because at least the pain reminds me that there once was someone inside here.

Virginia (*shakes her head*) You never ever said anything.

They sit there unspeaking.

Fade to blackout.

A couple of hours later.

The sun is now filling the room. **Diana** *is clearing things away. Sounds of a dog barking . . . a car door slams.*

Charlotte (*from upstairs*) Mum, I can't find my eye-shadow.

Diana You don't *need* your eye-shadow. You'll be in the car.

Virginia *enters.*

Virginia Darling, what are you doing?

Diana We're going.

Virginia It's only breakfast time.

Diana We'll have something on the way.

Virginia Why so early?

Diana Avoid the traffic.

Virginia I *know* why.

Diana Then why ask?

Alan *comes in from the hall, briskly.*

Alan I knew we shouldn't have left her in the car all night.

He disappears to the kitchen, from where we presently hear the sound of a bucket filling.

Virginia You came for the weekend.

Diana I think we've had the best of it.

Virginia You've never left so early before.

Diana I've never hated every minute of it before.

Charlotte *appears, looking indignant. She holds her make-up brush.*

Charlotte Mum! My make-up brush, he used it . . . as a toothbrush . . .

Diana Don't be ridiculous.

Charlotte He did . . . It was lying there. Beside his teeth.

Diana Have you got all your books?

Charlotte Why are we in such a hurry?

Alan *walks through from the kitchen with a bucket and a sponge.*

Alan She's been all over the instruction booklet . . . The car'll smell for weeks.

Charlotte (*to* **Alan**) Was Pippa in the car all night?

Diana (*to* **Charlotte**) Pack your bag and *stop* asking questions.

Charlotte You beast!

Alan Not my fault!

He exits through the front door, **Charlotte** *runs after him.*

Charlotte She's probably so frightened . . . Pippa! Pippa!

Diana (*yelling after* **Charlotte**) *Charlotte*! Don't shout! You'll wake Grandfather.

Stephen Grandfather's awake. He's had his hour and twenty minutes.

Stephen *comes into the room. He looks unusually cheerful.*

Virginia Oh, go back to bed dear . . . you *shouldn't* be up yet.

Stephen I don't like to miss a sunny day. We get few enough of them God knows . . . Want a hand?

He takes the tray from **Virginia** *and carries it into the kitchen.*

Virginia (*to* **Diana**, *suddenly and seriously*) Don't go . . .

Stephen (*off*) It's going to be quite a day! Perhaps we could take Charlotte to see Thorpeness Castle, then on the little railway . . . if it's really nice.

He reappears.

Diana (*exchanging a look with her mother*) We're leaving . . .

Stephen Oh. (*A pause.*) Going before lunch?

Diana No . . . before breakfast. (*She bustles past him and goes out.*)

Stephen Well, if she wants to go . . .

Virginia Yes, if she wants to go . . .

Stephen I thought . . . well I thought . . . well that's why I got up . . .

Diana *comes in again. She has* **Charlotte**'s *bag.*

Diana Anything we've left, we've left . . . we'll . . .

Virginia Get it next weekend.

Diana *nods mutely. The nearest she can get to meaning no, whilst saying yes.*

Diana Bye, Mum . . . Thanks for having us.

She kisses her, then she picks up the bag.

Bye, Dad . . .

She kisses him briskly.

Alan *comes in with the bucket.*

Alan She must have been terrified!

Charlotte *bounds back into the room and faces* **Stephen** *accusingly.*

Charlotte How would you like to have claustrophobia . . . *all* night.

Stephen Seventy-five cubic feet. Enough for a herd of camels.

Alan *goes into the kitchen. He empties the bucket.*

Diana (*to* **Charlotte**) Here's your bag.

Charlotte Have you packed everything?

Diana (*bustling out to the hallway*) Yes.

Virginia Next time . . . we'll make some room . . . in the shed perhaps.

Stephen I didn't force her to sleep in the bloody car.

Virginia (*to* **Charlotte**) What are you looking for?

Charlotte My magazine. It was here last night.

Stephen Probably disappeared in the clearing-up Olympics.

Charlotte It's *Seventeen*. It's the new one. I hadn't finished reading it.

Virginia I'll look for it.

Diana *comes back from the hall.*

Diana Come on you two!

Alan *comes out of the kitchen.*

Alan I've rinsed out the bucket . . . it's on the draining board.

Virginia Thank you, Alan.

Alan Goodbye, Virginia.

He gives her an awkward peck on the cheek.

Virginia You'll be here next weekend?

Diana (*before* **Alan** *can answer*) We'll see how things turn out.

Charlotte Bye Granny. (*She kisses her.*)

Virginia (*to* **Charlotte**) The ducks'll be nesting on the pond in a few days. You must help me get it ready for them.

Charlotte I'm going to Florida.

Virginia What?

Alan It's a school exchange. All done through Atlantic Air. Fifteen per cent reduction on an off-peak, Apex fare. They practically pay them to travel.

Virginia Maybe the weekend after . . .

Charlotte Going for two weeks. Bye, Grandad . . . (*She kisses him.*)

Diana (*at the door*) Come on . . . hurry up . . . and bring Pippa.

Alan It's all right . . . she's in the car.

Diana She's not in the car . . . I saw her going into the house.

Alan Oh no . . . !

*Everyone, except, strangely enough, **Stephen**, is galvanised into action. They turn and run upstairs. Barking and shouts are heard, a loud 'oh no!' and **Alan**'s admonitions.*

Stephen *stands awhile, then walks round the room. He sees something on a bookcase.*

They come down, all looking guilty: **Charlotte** *runs out carrying the dog.*

Alan Grandpa has to sleep on that!

Charlotte Don't shout at me! She only does it when she's unhappy!

Diana Shut up the two of you! (*To* **Virginia**.) I'm sorry.

Virginia It'll wash out.

Stephen Di –

Diana (*forestalling the inevitable*) It's all right! We'll put her in kennels next time.

Stephen I've found Charlotte's magazine.

He holds it out. **Diana** *stops her bustling momentarily, then takes the magazine.*

Diana Thanks, Daddy.

A smile flickers between them. She kisses him again, but thinks about it this time. Then turns and with a short wave makes for the front door. **Stephen** *turns to* **Virginia**.

Stephen Coming to see them off?

Virginia *shakes her head.*

Virginia No . . . no . . . you go.

Stephen *follows* **Diana** *out to the front door.* **Virginia** *goes across to the window and looks out at her departing family. She stands without moving for a moment. Then she turns, fighting tears, and automatically picks up a couple of dirty glasses. Then, unable for once to keep moving, she sits down on the sofa.*

Stephen *enters. He sniffs and takes a deep breath, then attempts a smile to* **Virginia**.

Stephen Cup of tea?

Virginia *makes to get up, but* **Stephen** *raises his hands.*

Stephen No . . . no . . . I'll get it.

Virginia's *head slowly turns from* **Stephen**, *as if not altogether sure she's heard aright. In the kitchen* **Stephen** *fills the kettle and plugs it in. He opens a cupboard door to look for the tea. Then another . . . and another.* **Stephen** *slowly goes through every cupboard, drawer and shelf, before finally giving up. He comes back into the room and up to* **Virginia**.

Stephen Where is it?

Virginia *can control herself no longer. She greets this with a marvellous, releasing laugh.*

Curtain.

www.ingramcontent.com/pod-product-compliance
Ingram Content Group UK Ltd.
Pitfield, Milton Keynes, MK11 3LW, UK
UKHW040639280225
455688UK00001B/8